THE BIRDS OF
JOHN BURROUGHS

John Burroughs at Woodchuck Lodge

THE BIRDS OF JOHN BURROUGHS

Keeping a Sharp Lookout

Edited and with an Introduction
by Jack Kligerman

Foreword by Dean Amadon

with drawings by Louis Agassiz Fuertes

HAWTHORN BOOKS, INC.
Publishers / NEW YORK

A Note on the Text

The essays are reprinted from the Riverby Edition of *The Writings of John Burroughs*. References below are to the book title, volume number, and page number. See Perry D. Westbrook's *John Burroughs* (Twayne, 1974) for a chronological listing of the first editions of the specific volumes. Burroughs's essays often had their genesis in journal entries or in letters to friends. The finished essays were first published in magazines, then, after various kinds of revisions, were collected for book publication. The Riverby Edition contains the final word.

THE BIRDS OF JOHN BURROUGHS

Library of Congress Catalog Card Number: 75–41803
ISBN: hardcover, 0–8015–0646–8; softcover, 0–8015–0647–6
1 2 3 4 5 6 7 8 9 10

To
Barbara,
Jonathan, and Rachel

CONTENTS

ILLUSTRATIONS

The drawings included in this volume were all done by Louis
Agassiz Fuertes and appeared in the Riverby Edition of *The
Writings of John Burroughs*.

FOREWORD

John Burroughs stated that his first book,[1] *Wake-Robin*, was an introduction to the study of birds. But even at that early phase of his career, his interests were wider, and the book is by no means exclusively taken up with this branch of natural history. The title, it is hardly necessary to say, is the name not of a bird but of a wild flower. Burroughs was not then and never became interested in writing manuals or handbooks. Rather he was an essayist, one whose subjects embraced not only the world of nature but also much of rural husbandry as well. The wild strawberry, the cow, the apple tree, gave him scope for meditation. His only other major field was literary criticism, notably as an early champion of Whitman, but also with lengthy critiques of Carlyle and others. The titles of Burroughs's books, chosen after much thought, are always felicitous and are to be taken symbolically— "Under the Maples," "Locusts and Wild Honey," "Signs and Seasons," "Harvest of the Years."

Nevertheless, when all is said and done, birds did hold a particular place in John Burroughs's esteem— both as a naturalist and a poet. He would have agreed with his friend Frank Chapman that birds are "nature's highest expression of beauty, joy, and truth."

1. Aside from an excessively rare little volume defending the poetry of his friend Walt Whitman.

FOREWORD

As we know from his journals, Burroughs was often of a melancholy turn of mind. That this is so seldom evident in his writings is, one feels sure, because of the renewal of spirits he found in birds and the natural world in general—which, for most of his life, he was fortunate enough to have at his doorstep. In his efforts to balance the better against the more somber aspects of the human condition, birds certainly played a lifelong and positive role. Hence, if a selection of some aspect of Burroughs's voluminous writings was to be gathered into an anthology, birds provided a natural and appropriate subject.

The flavor of Burroughs's writings on birds may best be savored by browsing through Professor Kligerman's selections. In general, they are factual and detailed accounts—often narratives of actual observations, but again distillations of lifelong impressions. Though of a poetic cast of mind and the author of a number of poems about birds, Burroughs's prose is constrained; never is he beguiled by his subjects into wild flights of fancy or imagination.

Is he, then, "scientific"? One occasionally finds in Burroughs's writings complaints about "professional ornithologists." But the type that distressed him was the then prevalent individual who examined a bird over the sights of a gun and whose only use for a nest and eggs was as an addition to his cabinet of specimens. Many such, of course, were mere collectors, not scientists. Even those that were scientists had a singularly narrow view of things. The ornithologist of today is astonished to read in Robert Ridgway's introduction to his multi-volumed *Birds of*

North and Middle America that there are two branches of ornithology: "scientific," describing and classifying (naturally, what Ridgway himself was doing); and "popular," the basis for everything else. But it is the latter segment that provides 95 percent of today's scientific ornithology!

But when Burroughs found a naturalist, in whatever field, who was concerned with the living animal, its habits and habitat (to use a vogue word), he was pleased and appreciative. Some of them became his friends—Frank Chapman, the ornithologist; Clyde Fisher, the versatile naturalist who concluded his career as the first director of the Hayden Planetarium; and others.

Anyone familiar with the totality of Burroughs's writings cannot for a moment question his zeal to understand the universe about him—animate and inanimate. He embraced Darwin's theory of evolution; he argued with John Muir about the forces responsible for Yosemite Canyon to the point where their friendship was strained (and in the verdict of posterity Burroughs was nearer the truth than the geologist Muir). Nor did he spare himself in seeking to learn *facts*—spending great effort in digging out and unraveling the intricate burrow of chipmunk or weasel. With a friend he made a determined, renewed, and eventually successful effort to discover the nest, the first known to science, of the black-throated blue warbler.

But while scientific in outlook and from time to time the discoverer of new facts about wildlife, Burroughs was not a scientist. He did not organize his

FOREWORD

observations and publish them as technical contributions. Rather, they are scattered through his essays. On one of the few occasions when he wrote a book "to order," a short life of John James Audubon, he later regretted it, preferring a more random and varied approach, as he tells us in his journal. If the spirit moved him he would write an entire essay on one rather limited subject, but then turn to other fields, or perhaps, following Candide's advice, work in his vineyards until the muse returned. His books, for the most part, are collections of rather disparate essays that have in common only the underlying thread of nature in its various guises.

At the present time there are many, many people interested in birds, and nowhere is this more true than in the northeastern United States where John Burroughs spent his life. For that reason, if for no other, it was desirable to gather and to republish his charming accounts of birds; accounts now somewhat neglected because of the current deluge of printed material. Those who observe and study birds, at whatever level of competence, will derive profit and pleasure from the pages of the Sage of Slabsides.

DEAN AMADON, President
The John Burroughs Association

THE BIRDS OF
JOHN BURROUGHS

INTRODUCTION

And in a launde, upon an hil of floures,
Was set this noble goddesse Nature.
Of braunches were here halles and here boures
Iwrought after here cast and here mesure;
Ne there nas foul that cometh of engendrure
That they ne were prest in here presence,
To take hire dom and yeve hire audyence.
                              —Geoffrey Chaucer
                              The Parliament of Fowls

Several years ago my family and I went backpacking
with friends up Slide Mountain, the highest peak in
the Catskills, in New York State. It was late May,
and home, which lies in Closter, New Jersey, had
already begun its quick move into summer. We spent
one night in Woodland Valley, to the north, and on
a Saturday morning began the hike around to the
west, from which direction we were to make our
climb. Of course, as we moved up in space, we moved
back in seasonal time. Vegetation thinned out until
only buds were left on the hardwoods and adder's-
tongues had not yet begun to blossom. It was a
brilliant day, and the cool air kept the hiking com-

fortable. On top we set up camp, watched a beautiful sunset, then ate under a brighter star-studded sky than we had seen since camping in Tuolumne meadows, in the Yosemite, when our children were very young. Now they could carry their own packs. And before dinner they could help us get water by scrambling down the 250-foot drop to the spring, near the beginning of the trail from Slide Mountain summit to Cornell and Wittenberg mountains. On our way back up, before we turned left toward the campsite, we saw a plaque on the face of a large rock outcropping that formed a natural shelter. The plaque bore the name of John Burroughs. We carried this fact back along with the water, spent a fine evening, and went to sleep anticipating another clear day with almost limitless landscapes.

We woke up early to one of the most bitter winds and driving rainstorms that we had ever experienced. Something had betrayed us. At first we thought it was nature being as indifferent as ever and, from the vantage of human comforts, as cruel. But nature had not done the betraying. The signs of change had been everywhere about us, day and night. If we had been better instructed to read what we saw, we might not have been taken so by surprise.

It was only several years later that I finally learned what we had needed to know. I found the following advice in John Burroughs's essay, "A Sharp Lookout": "When the atmosphere is telescopic, and distant objects stand out unusually clear and sharp, a storm is near. . . . In this state of the atmosphere the stars are unusually numerous and bright at night,

which is also a bad omen."[1] It was no consolation to
the memory of our chilled bones to learn, also much
later, that Burroughs himself had been caught by a
storm on Slide Mountain in 1885, where he had gone
camping with his neighbors, the Van Benschotens,
and his friend, a farmer and writer, Myron Benton:
"We were now not long in squaring an account with
Slide, and making ready to leave. Round pellets of
snow began to fall, and we came off the mountain
on the 10th of June in a November storm and temperature."[2] So Slide Mountain was still the same, and
John Burroughs was discovered to be a veritable
human being. I had met him, as it were, both on the
mountain and in his books.

It was an auspicious set of coincidences that had
led up to this meeting: John Burroughs on Slide
Mountain over a hundred years before I got there,
camping above the spring under that natural shelter
where I came across his name; my finding a reference
in one of his essays that detailed circumstances so
like those I had encountered; and my curiosity being
quickened by the insight of a man who could both see
the world around him and read what he saw. And
so, looking back, I can think of no better way to have
begun our acquaintance. Though John Burroughs
long ago became part of the mountain earth that he
loved, something of his spirit can yet be found everywhere, if one's perception is keen enough to spot it.

Perhaps some of the best places to look for John
Burroughs is where people for decades past have
found him: in his essays on birds. These essays are
remarkable for their appreciation of the birds them-

selves as well as for their understanding of the many significant connections between birds and men, which he explores with an undying curiosity and fertile simplicity. As he wrote in an essay, "The Summit of the Years," in 1911, still ten years from the end of his long career as essayist, naturalist, and farmer, "The live bird is a fellow passenger; we are making the voyage together, and there is a sympathy between us that quickly leads to knowledge" (*Writings*, XVII, 13).

John Burroughs's eighty-four-year journey began on April 3, 1837, in a farmhouse near Roxbury, New York, where he spent his first seventeen years. His grandparents, Eden Burroughs and Rachel Avery, had moved into this virgin land in the Catskills in 1795, cutting themselves a road through the woods to where they made a clearing and built their log cabin. His father was born on this land in 1803. His mother's history is similar, blending into the myth of westward expansion that has permeated the American imagination since before Thomas Jefferson. In 1826, Burroughs's parents bought a neighboring farm and settled in to raising crops, cattle, and ten children, of whom John was the seventh. By the time he was born, the landscape had adopted its idyllic pastoral pose that can yet be found at places in the Catskills. A testimony of the land's typical peacefulness, its distance from "unhandselled" savage nature and wilderness, can be found everywhere in the paintings of those nineteenth-century artists who came to be known as the Hudson River School. Burroughs's father was in fact a contemporary of Thomas Cole

and Asher Brown Durand, while Burroughs himself
was the contemporary of the second wave of these
painters: Albert Bierstadt, Frederick Church, John
F. Kensett, and Thomas Moran. Burroughs grew up,
in other words, when the first hewing of a life out of
the wilderness was over. One still needed to respect
nature, but one no longer needed to fear it. People
had begun to look scientifically at the natural world.
In fact, Darwin had come back from his voyage on
the *Beagle* a year before Burroughs was born. A major change in apprehending the concept of nature
was underway. One could now lie back, observe the
natural world, and discover what it was all about. Or
one could pursue it and hunt it down.

To be sure, life for a farmer and his family in the
nineteenth century was not easy. But the homestead
made nature accessible to John Burroughs. It gave
him pleasant associations that would last a lifetime
and freely granted him an ever present field of study.
He would come back to Roxbury during the summers
throughout his later years. And he would take his
love for nature with him wherever he went. As late
as May 7, 1917, a month after his eightieth birthday,
he noted in his journal, "Very wet and chilly. Only
grass can grow. . . . Many myrtle warblers here. . . .
My hunger for nature unabated" (*Life*, II, 251). He
would thus link, in even this casual comment, two
of the three major forces in his intellectual and emotional development: the farm and the birds. The
third force was literature.

On the farm Burroughs came to know intimately
all forms of wildlife, from frogs to bees, from birds to

chipmunks; and he breathed in, one might say, a farmer's antipathy to woodchucks that would stay with him to the end. He would also go strawberrying and apple picking; he would hoe corn, dig potatoes, and thresh oats in the same barn that in later years would serve him as his hay-barn study, which he discusses in "A Hay-Barn Idyl." He would clear fields of stone, clean stables, and burn stumps; and he would store up memories of what was perhaps his favorite farm chore: maple sugar-making in March, the first spring work: "Next week, or the week after, it may be time to begin plowing, and other sober work about the farm; but this week we will picnic among the maples, and our campfire shall be an incense to spring" (*Writings*, II, 104). Burroughs also valued the chore because it would take him to the woods, where he could hear the robins' "merry calls" once again. A pure, sensual longing, associations and curiosity, the past and the present, human life and natural facts and, above all, their intermingling permitted a perfect balance. All these are the legacies of his childhood, which he would draw upon for the rest of his life. Even at the age of seventy-eight, he would set down in his journal words symbolic of the enduring qualities of life on the farm: March 31, 1916, "I sit here boiling sap, sparrow songs all about me."[3]

Burroughs had little formal schooling. The only degrees he received were honorary ones granted him late in life by Yale, Colgate, and the University of Georgia. Unlike his precursors in writing about nature, Ralph Waldo Emerson and Henry David Thoreau, there was no Harvard for him until his son

Julian went there in 1897. Perhaps this is why Burroughs had no need to discover nature or to uncover it to find another, more satisfying reality. Nature was first a fact for Burroughs and only afterwards a concept. It never became for him the total symbol of spirit as it was for Emerson. To be sure, the earlier writer was a major influence in Burroughs's life, and echoes of Emerson reverberate throughout his essays. Nevertheless, the orientation of Emerson's thinking was different. Drawing on centuries of neo-Platonic thought, Emerson could assert in *Nature*, "Every natural fact is a symbol of some spiritual fact."[4] Emerson valued particular phenomena in nature primarily as vehicles of a language expressive of mind and spirit. Burroughs, however, tempted as he often might be by a transcendental impulse, nevertheless loved the facts of nature—birds, flowers, even the soil—for themselves. He wrote in the essay "The Divine Soil," "The lesson which life repeats and constantly enforces is 'look under foot.' You are always nearer the divine and the true sources of your power than you think" (*Writings*, XXIII, 286). In locating primary value in the world of natural phenomena, Burroughs turns topsy-turvy the world view of the transcendentalists, an achievement that forms what is perhaps his greatest contribution to the natural history essay in America.

The lack of formal schooling permitted Burroughs a fertile ground for his philosophic materialism. He wrote in the essay "Mere Egotism," published in *Lippincott's Magazine* in 1886 and reprinted as "An Egotistical Chapter" in the volume *Indoor Studies*

(1889), "In my own case, at least, what I needed most was what I had—a few books and plenty of real things" (*Writings*, VIII, 264). He did attend the local West Settlement school as a child, though, and when in his eighteenth year he managed to eke out some months at the Hedding Literary Institute in Greene County. He turned teacher himself at a country school in Tongore, New York, where he earned enough money to attend the Cooperstown Seminary during the spring term of 1856. But the intermittent pattern of both his schooling and his teaching serves to reinforce the sense that nature was his best tutor. Though there is always a danger inherent in attributing aspects of one's style to one's background, major pitfalls might be avoided at this point by allowing Henry James the floor. "Mr. Burroughs is known as an out-of-door observer—a devotee of birds and trees and fields and aspects of weather and humble wayside incidents. The minuteness of his observations, the keenness of his perception of all these things, give him a real originality which is confirmed by a style sometimes indeed idiomatic and unfinished to a fault, but capable of remarkable felicity and vividness."[5] Whenever faced with a choice of priorities, Burroughs would always cast his lot with this world, the world of natural facts, of real things. He would have no other choice.

Burroughs's position in American literature, vis-à-vis the natural history essay and an understanding of nature as a concept, is therefore unique. He could not be a lover of *wildness* or *wilderness*, in Thoreau's apprehension of these terms, because his childhood associations with nature were pastoral. He had no need to romanticize the woods because he had no need in his formative years to escape a city upbringing. In addition, the intimate, close-up knowledge of nature that he learned in his youth prevented him from being sympathetic with the idealistic, conceptualized, middle-distance view of nature, which was essentially the vantage point of the Hudson River School. Nor could he accept either the allegorizing tendency of Thomas Cole or the conceptually abstract imagery of the tradition of the sublime, the picturesque, and the beautiful which was current in the aesthetic conventions of his time, in both painting and poetry. If any developments in art in nineteenth-century America parallel Burroughs's sense of the world, they can be found in the precise, detailed work in the paintings of birds by Alexander Wilson and John James Audubon. In fact, the stylistic similarities between Burroughs and Audubon were, as we shall soon see, no accident.

In growing up, Burroughs had kept company with the source, with his "divine soil." He now began to keep company with a young woman, Ursula North, of Olive, New York. He married her on September 12, 1857. Soon his life and his education were to take a new turn. According to Clara Barrus, Burroughs's biographer, Ursula North was a woman "who had preëminently certain traits in which he was deficient, notably pride, self-confidence, and aggressiveness" (*Life*, I, 45). She asked what a wife could reasonably demand of a husband: some place to set up house where she could come to live with him. So Burroughs continued to teach, moving in 1858 to East Orange, New Jersey, where by February of the following year, his financial situation enabled Ursula to join him. Meanwhile, he had begun to write seriously, sending articles to the *Saturday Press*, a New York weekly that had published poems of Walt Whitman's, and to the *New York Leader*. In the November 1860 issue of the *Atlantic Monthly*, which he subscribed to all his life, he published an essay entitled "Expression" that was "so Emersonian in tone that [James Russell] Lowell, then editor, looked through all of Emerson's published work before [being] convinced that it was not a plagiarism" (*Life*, I, 52). Burroughs had found his milieu but not yet his métier. By the fall of 1860 he was back in New York State, teaching at Marlboro-on-the-Hudson, writing a series of essays for the *New York Leader* called, appropriately, "From the Back Country." Still spending his summers at work on the home farm, in December 1862 he took a job teaching at Highland Falls, New York, then named Buttermilk Falls, and tried to study medicine. But by the spring of 1863 he gave it up; he had discovered wild flowers. Things were beginning to fit in place.

In June 1863, Burroughs experienced an encounter that eventually turned him into the writer of the essays in this book. This meeting took place in the library of West Point. Burroughs came upon a copy of Audubon's *The Birds of America*. Although one finds references throughout his essays on birds to Alexander Wilson's *American Ornithology*, first published in Philadelphia (1808–1814), and to Thomas

12

INTRODUCTION

Nuttall's *Manual of the Ornithology of the United States and Canada* (1832–1834), it was Audubon's monumental work that reoriented Burroughs's imagination and gave him a vocation. In Audubon's paintings one sees not just the bird itself, but occasionally the environment, usually the specific, immediate habitat, and often the natural food of the bird depicted. Furthermore, Audubon was not just an ornithologist but also an artist. His representations are meticulously detailed and designed with an eye to the harmony of images. Even if Audubon employed, according to Robert Henry Welker, "the middle distance and background vistas" on some prints when presenting "ground, shore, and water birds," in virtually all his paintings the foreground contains "the principal subject, the bird, and generally all other important decorative motives. It is perhaps his use of essentially flat, close-up patterns which gives his paintings much of their impact and sense of immediacy." Moreover, with Audubon "the observer knows quite clearly where he is situated; that is, always close-up and at eye level with the bird, whether it be on the ground, in low briers, perched among flowers, high in a tree, or flying far over the earth. In effect, the bird is not moved into place for the observer, but the other way around, for the world is not anthropocentric but ornithocentric."[6]

Burroughs was captivated. By the end of July he was rereading an essay in the *Atlantic Monthly* of December 1858 by Wilson Flagg entitled "The Birds of the Pasture and the Forest," and while camping in the Adirondacks in August, he was gathering mental notes and inspiration for one of his first nature essays, "With the Birds," which was published in the *Atlantic Monthly* in the spring of 1865. In a revised form it became the first chapter of Burroughs's first book on nature subjects, *Wake-Robin*, published in 1871. John Burroughs was on his way.

To see birds, to record them accurately, precisely, to set them in relation to their habitat, to see them in connection with man in general and his perceptive consciousness in particular—these became the lessons Burroughs was to learn from Audubon. In retrospect, Burroughs would write, "Studied the birds? No, I have played with them, camped with them, gone berrying with them, summered and wintered with them, and my knowledge of them has filtered into my mind almost unconsciously" (*Writings*, XVII, 13). He did more than all this, however. He came to love them. But it was a love that shifted the center of the universe for Burroughs. He later observed, "Life seems only an incident in the universe, evidently not an end" (*Writings*, XVI, 269). To be sure, this is post-evolutionary thinking, but Burroughs's understanding of wildlife, enhanced by Audubon's work, prepared him for his eventual acceptance of Darwinism. When the time came, he therefore admitted man's absence at the center of any universal design, though he was always unwilling to admit consciously that the "manward impulse" was not the direction toward which all life was tending. As he wrote in 1912, "I am sure I was an evolutionist in the abstract, or by the quality and complexion of my mind, before I read Darwin, but to become an evolutionist in the concrete, and accept the doctrine of the animal origin of man, has not for me been an easy matter" (*Writings*, XVI, vi). No other theory besides evolution, however, can account for the inspiration of the following quotation: "We are rooted to the air through our lungs and to the soil through our stomachs. We are walking trees and floating plants" (*Writings*, XV, 200).

To repeat, Burroughs's modern understanding of man's place in life came to him partly through his encounter with Audubon. He learned what he must have already intuited, that there was another world out there outside of consciousness, a world of birds, a world of fascinating creatures that was independent of the mind of God or man. Thus, what is permanent in Burroughs's essays is his ability to penetrate into the very essence of the birds themselves. At such moments, self disappears and words come as close as they can to dissolving. Within the limits of his language, as Audubon within the limits of his medium and his vision, Burroughs was to begin offering in his nature essays "a careful and conscientious record of actual observations and experiences" (*Writings*, I, v). Along with John Muir, whom he would meet later in life, Burroughs was about to begin to become one of the "outstanding American prose writers on nature" since Thoreau. "Set apart by their union of scientific accuracy with the power of expression," wrote Norman Foerster of Burroughs and Muir in *Nature in American Literature*, "these two writers have established a virtually new type of literature, the nature essay."[7]

THE BIRDS OF JOHN BURROUGHS

One could not predict, in the library at West Point that June day in 1863, what the upshot of Burroughs's encounter with Audubon would be. What is clear, however, is that Burroughs had discovered a subject as well as an aesthetic model, even if the medium was different from that which he had chosen for his future. What could also not be predicted was the next sudden change of events in Burroughs's life.

In September 1863 Burroughs wrote, "I am getting dissatisfied and crave action. . . . I do want to get nearer to this bugbear, War!" (*Life*, I, 80). Disaffected with teaching and forced to look for a better position by the simple economics of housekeeping, Burroughs turned up in Washington, D.C., in 1863, found a temporary job in the quartermaster general's department, and wrote to his wife that he had met Whitman. He was to become the poet's lifelong friend, early defender, and companion in many walks in and around the capital for the next nine years.

Burroughs and Whitman had much in common. They were both children of farmers. They both came from large families. Their education had been in early life anything but the best. They were both great walkers. They were curious. And they loved nature not in the abstract but in its very particulars. Whitman, of course, had almost twenty years on Burroughs, who was fast to become his disciple. What Burroughs found in Whitman, however, that perhaps drew him so quickly to the poet, crops up in one of the younger man's journal entries. In writing of Whitman's eyes on August 26, 1865, he says, "I occasionally see something in them, as he bends them upon me, that almost makes me draw back. . . . It is as if the Earth looked at me . . . (*Journals*, 41). There was more, though. There was the joy of the immediacy of sense impressions and the value of interfering as little as possible in the translation of these impressions into language and literature. They were keen observers. And they understood something about nature that Whitman described thus:

> I believe a leaf of grass is no less than the
>   journeywork of the stars,
> And the pismire is equally perfect, and a grain
>   of sand, and the egg of the wren.[8]

Moreover, what they understood in common, Burroughs and Whitman, was that the proper attitude of man toward nature should be humility. Only then was love possible. And only through love could one gain a true appreciation of the natural world and of man's place in it.

Burroughs and Whitman also shared certain literary values, some of which appear throughout Burroughs's essays on birds. Or perhaps one should rather say that Burroughs saw both simplicity and total acceptance at the heart of Whitman's self. These values, allied to what Burroughs had found in Audubon's paintings, helped form an aesthetic for the nature essay. But neither Burroughs nor Whitman could know the ubiquity of what they had hit upon. One finds the following in the writings of Bashō, a seventeenth-century Japanese poet and master of haiku: "Go to the pine if you want to learn about the

17

pine, or to the bamboo if you want to learn about the bamboo. And in doing so, you must leave your subjective preoccupation with yourself. Otherwise you impose yourself on the object and do not learn. Your poetry issues of its own accord when you and the object have become one—when you have plunged enough into the object to see something like a hidden glimmering there."[9]

All his life Burroughs had gone to the woods and fields. He knew that there were "few better places to study ornithology than in the orchard" (*Writings*, II, 138). And he knew what he was looking for: "free and ungarnered harvests which the wilderness everywhere affords to the observing eye and ear" (*Writings*, IV, Preface). But now he knew also that he had to let the birds flow through him and to record what he saw and felt as simply as possible. These became his goals. They constitute his value: "The sensations of the first day are what we want,—the first flush of the traveller's thought and feeling, before his perception and sensibilities become cloyed or blunted, or before he in any way becomes a part of that which he would observe and describe" (*Writings*, II, v).

But Whitman helped supply Burroughs with a stylistic ideal as well as with a vision. In fact, the two overlapped. In the preface of the 1855 edition of *Leaves of Grass*, Whitman had indicated what he believed was the necessary attitude of the writer toward his language: "The greatest poet has less a marked style and is more the channel of thoughts and things without increase and diminution, and is the free channel of himself. . . . What I experience or portray shall go from my composition without a shred of my composition."[10] Quoting this passage years later in the essay "Style and the Man," Burroughs would add: "The great success in writing is to get language out of the way and to put your mind directly to the reader's, so that there be no veil of words between you. . . . Words are like lenses,—they must be arranged in just such a way, or they hinder rather than help the vision. When the adjustment is as it should be, the lens itself is invisible" (*Writings*, XII, 74). Throughout his essays Burroughs works toward this impossible ideal. He gives himself entirely to his subject and, in a language simple and generally unmetaphorical, allows his readers to consider the subjects directly with as little interference as possible.

Burroughs stayed in Washington, D.C. for nine years. He built a house, cultivated a garden, became a treasury clerk at the currency bureau, ate huge oyster dinners with Whitman, invited him regularly for Ursula's Sunday pancake breakfasts, and published both his own first book and the first book to be written on Whitman, *Notes on Walt Whitman as Poet and Person*, based on his article "Walt Whitman and his Drum Taps," which appeared in *The Galaxy* in December 1866. He wrote often now. While at work on the Whitman essay, he was finishing one called "Snow Walkers" and another, "In the Hemlocks." This last contains the passage on the hermit thrush that apparently inspired Whitman to choose this bird for use in his elegy to Lincoln, "When Lilacs Last in the Dooryard Bloom'd." Burroughs described the song of the hermit thrush as "the voice of that calm, sweet solemnity one attains to in his best moments. It realizes a peace and a deep, solemn joy that only the finest souls may know" (*Writings*, I, 52).

By now Burroughs had his characteristic material for essays: literature, aspects of rural life and life in the backwoods, and birds. Though later on his reading would embrace scientific and philosophical subjects, and though he occasionally would threaten to have finished writing on birds, he constantly would be drawn back to his original interests. The essays reprinted in this text alone span fifty-five years. To be sure, Whitman did not give Burroughs his subjects, but the poet did provide the younger man with a perspective from which to see their possibilities. Reminiscing on the force of Whitman in his life, Burroughs would say: "I owe more to him than to any other man in the world. He brooded me; he gave me things to think of; he taught me generosity, breadth, and an all-embracing charity. . . . The indirect, orbicular style of the Leaves—he talked in the same way—his talk always suggestive—'Not to finish specimens, but to shower them, as Nature does'" (*Life*, I, 113).

"Not to finish specimens"! This might be too much like shooting and stuffing birds, an occupation that Burroughs admittedly shared with Audubon and other early ornithologists but which was necessary for scientists in the middle of the nineteenth century. Burroughs would afterwards gladly prefer "a small field-glass to a gun" (*Writings*, I, 221, footnote). With patience he would train himself to blend into the environment when in the field, and, unless his pursuits demanded otherwise, would disturb the birds as little as possible while looking about him. In turning his mental notes into journal entries and the material for essays, he would try to give his reader "a live bird and not a labelled specimen" (*Writings*, I, xvi). There would remain often something of the unfinished about his essays. Nature, as he said in the essay "Gay Plumes and Dull," "would not be tabulated" (*Writings*, XV, 67). Thus one looks in vain throughout Burroughs's prose for the artificially organic, totally circumscribed whole. His essays have the kind of open-endedness that one finds in the winter woods, not the shape that one finds in individual trees or in many of the journal entries of Thoreau.

In fact, the closest approximation for a specific literary form among Burroughs's contemporaries can be found in the poems of Whitman. In these and Burroughs's essays, one notices the details of the writers' perceptions, follows the line of their vision, and turns away from the apprehended subject when the writer turns away. So if Burroughs's writing strikes one as not neatly packaged or wrapped up in the spirit of one's mind, recall that it is designed to let quite a different kind of life-spirit flow through.

Burroughs's essays share other aspects of Whitman's poetry besides their form. He uses catalogs to shape his observations, both within paragraphs and between them. The motion is the sweep of his eye, or very often his ear, as he seeks to find the elusive prey that has caught his curiosity. And along with the catalog as an organizing principle comes repetition. This, like any aspect of style or the patterned use of language, is more than a mere device, however. Repetition in both Burroughs's and Whitman's writings constitutes a philosophic point of view that insists on the equality of all things and the timelessness of repeated forms of life. Repetition is very much the analogue in style for what Burroughs in one of his late essays calls the "master instinct": "From the naturalist's point of view, the sole purpose of all forms of life in this world, man included, is to beget more life, and secure the perpetuity of the species. The master instinct in every living creature is to increase and multiply and fill the world with its progeny" (*Writings*, XIX, 65). Another lesson learned through the master: "Urge and urge and urge,/Always the procreant urge of the world."[11] And so his essays do not end. They simply stop for a moment. "Is there an end to nature?" one almost hears John Burroughs asking.

Burroughs's years in Washington, D.C. were soon bound to come to a close. Often drawn back to his parents' homestead in Roxbury during the summers, in 1872 he resigned his position in the capital and came back to the Hudson Valley for good. He was given a job as a special bank examiner, which he kept until about 1885. He found a nine-acre farm on the west bank of the Hudson, not far below Esopus, New York, eighty miles or so from New York City and not far, even then, from his parents' farm near Roxbury. He bought the property on September 15, 1873. He would call it, quite appropriately, Riverby. Here he would settle in to as permanent a place as he was to know all his life. And here he would grow into the white-haired sage whose name I encountered on top of Slide Mountain. Riverby was the perfect place to settle for one of his interests. To the east was the river; not far to the west was higher, rockier ground, rising to ledges that overlooked the Hudson and then dipped, further west, to the small valley of the Shattega, or Black Creek, near where Burroughs would build Slabsides some twenty-odd years later. Slightly off to the southwest was Chodikee Lake, then called Black Pond. For the birdwatcher, many different environments were within easy walking distance: timbered marshland, woody streams, swamps, the shore of the Hudson and the Hudson River Valley flyway, hardwood forest areas and conifer woods, and Burroughs's own farmland with its orchards, vineyards, and various kinds of brush cover. It is interesting that even though Burroughs considered his buying the land for Slabsides as a purchase of a retreat into the wilderness, by the end of his first spring there he already had put in a garden and a considerable number of celery plants.[12]

Burroughs had found his native habitat. He would soon build his habitation, some of it with his own hands. He relished the stonework and selected much of the wood himself for the interior decoration. Writing a retrospective of fifty years of Burroughs's contributions to the *Atlantic Monthly*, Dallas Lore Sharp in 1910 developed the symbolic importance of settling in to the earth for Burroughs: "Here in the vineyard along the Hudson, Mr. Burroughs planted himself in planting his vines, and every trellis that he has set has become his own support and stay. The very clearing of the land for his vineyard was a preparation of himself physically and morally for a more fruitful life."[13] His life, planted so well in his home soil, could now sit back and attune itself to the seasons.

In addition, what he had placed himself in proximity to was what he called the "primal sanities" of nature (*Writings*, XVI, 253). The birds could be considered one of these: "If the bird has not preached to me, it has added to the resources of my life, it has widened the field of my interests, it has afforded me another beautiful object to love, and has helped me to feel more at home in this world" (*Writings*, XVI, 253). The seasons themselves were another: "One seems to get nearer to nature in the early spring days: all screens are removed, the earth everywhere speaks directly to you" (*Writings*, IX, 236). He had reconnected himself to his past and to the basic simplicities of life that governed him as a child. Yet, he was anything but naive. Where Thoreau, in all due respect, played the farmer with his beans, Burroughs worked the farm for his livelihood—the experiences yielded both survival and material for his essays. He knew how to wait, and he knew that to be an observer in the truest sense was to "find what you are not looking for" (*Writings*, XV, 6).

But at the same time Burroughs understood the harsh realities of farming. He wrote in his journal on September 20, 1892: "On Saturday, the 17th, the bottom went out of the grape-market, leaving me with two or three tons of Concords on the vines.

INTRODUCTION

These we are sending off slowly, and getting low prices. For the first time in nearly a week I can sit at my ease and look up at the serene sky" (*Journals*, 169). He also understood and was grateful for the rewards this new life was bringing him. The journal entry for March 23, 1901, reads: "In the morning a meadowlark alighted on top of the maple over my Study, and sent forth, again and again, his wonderful spring call. In the forenoon I worked on 'The Life of Audubon,' and in the afternoon boiled sap—six pails. The best sap yet. The white gulls go up the river, their images reflected in the water beneath them" (*Journals*, 225). Primal sanities and simplicity, the consciousness, almost the cadences of an imagist poet, or of Ralph Waldo Emerson.

These latter qualities can be found everywhere in the language of Burroughs's essays. Although Burroughs would acknowledge a debt to Emerson and Thoreau in a precise use of metaphor and other forms of analogy, it is rather the briefness and directness of Emerson's essays that Burroughs found congenial to his mind. Emerson provided him with a model of effective short sentences, with a self-confident, assertive tone, with the force of aphorisms, and with a reinforcement of what Wordsworth called in his preface to the *Lyrical Ballads* (1800) "the language really spoken by men." Moreover, repetition was an aspect of Emerson's style as well as Whitman's, especially in the repeated use of simple sentences and noun clusters, specifically ones with a parallel syntactic structure. Yet it was not just sentence structure that Burroughs perceived in Emerson's essays. It was also a vocabulary. Though Emerson tends to use more abstractions than any other nineteenth-century American writer on nature, he also established firmly the value of concreteness. In fact, Emerson's typical metaphor was located in noun phrases fashioned out of a combination of concrete and abstract nouns: for example, the "knapsack of custom." And often, when the subject noun was an abstraction, Emerson would counterbalance this weight with a concrete verb: "All promise *outruns* the performance."[14] Burroughs would use a much more abstract vocabulary in his literary or philosophical essays, but in his essays on birds he would value the concreteness of Emerson's language: "Probably that language is the most suggestive that is the most concrete, that is drawn most largely from the experience of life, that savors of real things" (*Writings*, XII, 237).

This language, then, is the language of Burroughs's nature essays—more often than not, straightforward and simple. Even when he allows metaphor to structure his portrait of birds or animals, his framework of interpretation comes from domestic life, farm life, or some other kind of daily human activity. He eschews paradox for the simplicity of readily apparent analogies. And if he does find the need to use paradox, interpretation is never a puzzle. There is no end to the wisdom of a bird's nest. Simplicity and function. Naturalness. These are the impressions of Burroughs's style. As Walt Whitman said in 1888, "John's power is in his simplicity. He writes well because he does not try to write. . . . He never bowls you over with any vivid passion of speech—it is not in him to do it—but he calms you and soothes you—takes you out into the open where things are in an amiable mood."[15]

These are also one's impressions of Burroughs's life at Riverby, which in the 1870s and 1880s stretched out in time with the regularity of the seasons, always the same yet always, like the seasons, different. In his essays he recorded the seasons as they passed and the birds that followed the seasons in their great migrations north and south. He built a separate study at Riverby, the Bark-Study, which he finished in 1882 and which is still standing today. It and Slabsides, also still standing but then yet to come, were declared National Historic Landmarks on May 24, 1969. To be sure, he continued to tramp the woods, making mental notes of what came across him, but business at home, both in the field and in the study, were more than enough to keep him occupied. His hair and beard turned white, and he now looked the part of the sage that his growing audience had cast him in. He had his bees, he raised chickens, he tended his orchards and the crops of fruit and birds that each year grew with its branches. Chickadees, woodpeckers, screech owls would nest in the old trees. Each spring brought back the bluebirds, the robins, the orioles, and the wrens. But the passenger pigeons, after 1876, would not come back to the Hudson Valley, at least not to be seen by John Burroughs. They would soon disappear from the earth itself. He learned to face the challenge of the familiar: "I consider myself lucky if, in the course of a season, I can pick up two or three facts in natural history that are new to me. To have a new delight in an old and familiar face is not always easy, and is perhaps quite as much to be desired. The familiar we always have with us; to see it with fresh eyes so as to find a new pleasure in it,—that is a great point" (*Writings*, XIII, 191).

Ever restless, though, and always filled with new projects, in 1888 on eight newly acquired acres, he put in a new vineyard with raspberries and currant bushes. Wrens and bluebirds moved in quickly. Warblers would fascinate him in the spring, as they "followed" the insects northward, and would challenge him with their confusing plumages in the fall. They would never cease to draw him. In fact it was Burroughs who recorded the first finding of the nest of the worm-eating warbler in New York State, as well as that of other species. During these years at Riverby, what he had felt as a long solitude was coming to a close. Visitors came often to his home on the Hudson—too often, one suspects, for by the end of 1895 he had bought the land to the west and by spring of 1896 had set up his new study and retreat at Slabsides. He had once again, as it were, moved in with the birds. In "Wild Life about My Cabin" he tells of this removal and what he found there. The details of Burroughs's life as it worked its way toward the twentieth century do not need to be recounted here, however. Beginning in 1876, Burroughs diligently kept a journal, much of which was reprinted by Clara Barrus in her *Life and Letters of John Burroughs* and in her selection in *The Heart of Burroughs's Journals*. Burroughs's granddaughter, Mrs. Elizabeth Burroughs Kelley, still lives on the

INTRODUCTION

family property at Riverby and has eloquently retold the story of John Burroughs and his family in her book, *John Burroughs: Naturalist*. She also recently published, in addition, a specific, detailed account of her grandfather's life at Slabsides. What is important to note at this point is that Burroughs was still growing intellectually through his readings in Darwinism, geology, and Henri Bergson, to indicate several of the directions his interests were taking.

But Burroughs never lost his "faith in the eternal veracity of things" (*Writings*, XV, 255). He cultivated not only his garden but also what he considered the rarest of gifts, the power to see straight: "to see no more and no less than is actually before you; to be able to detach yourself and see the thing as it actually is, uncolored and unmodified by your own sentiments or prepossessions. In short, to see with your reason as well as your perceptions, that is to be an observer and to read the book of nature aright" (*Writings*, XIV, 238). Moreover he never forgot that "love is the measure of life: only so far as we love do we really live" (*Writings*, XV, 3).

Years would go by. He would become friends with John Muir, that other American naturalist who made his own trails in the Yosemite. He would go to Alaska in 1899 with the Harriman Expedition, where he first met the young Louis Agassiz Fuertes, who would be the illustrator for *The Writings of John Burroughs* when Houghton Mifflin published the Riverby edition of his writings in 1904. Fuertes, of course, would go on to become one of the most influential of all bird illustrators in American painting.

29

THE BIRDS OF JOHN BURROUGHS

Burroughs would go camping with Teddy Roosevelt, Henry Ford, and Thomas Edison. Many visitors, ornithologists in particular, would come to him both for his company and to share experiences with him in the field. His influence on the study of natural history became so great and lasting that even today there is a fine memorial in his honor in the Education Hall of the American Museum of Natural History. After his death in 1921, friends formed the John Burroughs Memorial Association, which is still active and which each year grants a medal to the best book published in the field of natural history upholding John Burroughs's tradition.

Yet, in spite of how much he was drawn into the world of men and women in his later years, he never lost his eye for birds. As he grew older, he would spend longer and longer periods at Woodchuck Lodge in the summer. This home had once belonged to his brother Curtis and neighbored on his parents' old farm near Roxbury. He would settle himself at a desk in the hay barn and write some of his last essays on birds. He was curious even in his eighties and still learning new things. On June 6, 1920, he wrote in his journal, "Discovered that the webs of the little spiders in the road, fairy napkins, saturated with minute drops of moisture, exhibit prismatic tints. In it we see one abutment of a tiny rainbow. Step a pace or two to the other side, and you see the other abutment. You never see the completed bow, because the web is too small" (*Journals*, 332). Woodchuck Lodge itself became a National Historic Landmark in 1963, and in 1966, nearby Memorial Field,

INTRODUCTION

where Burroughs is buried and where he played as a little boy, was dedicated as a New York State Historic Site. Even his later essays, "The Spring Bird Procession" and "Fuss and Feathers," share qualities that William Dean Howells noted in *Wake-Robin*, Burroughs's first book of nature essays: "His nerves have a poetical sensitiveness, his eye a poetical quickness; and many of his descriptive passages impart all the thrill of his subtle observation."[16] Bliss Perry, speaking in 1923 at the Burroughs Memorial Meeting of the American Academy of Arts and Letters, which had elected Burroughs a member in 1905 and had granted him its gold medal in 1916, praised Burroughs's shrewdness, which had brought him to investigate the questions, "How does the chipmunk dig his hole? And what does he do with the dirt?"[17] The curious naturalist to the very end. The art of the familiar and the wisdom of simplicity.

The birds, Burroughs's "fellow passengers" for so long a time, had become so much a part of his life that he wrote, "To take the birds out of my life would be like lopping off so many branches from the tree: there is so much less surface of leafage to absorb the sunlight and bring my spirits in contact with the vital currents" (*Writings*, XVI, 253). The wonder that the world held for him for eighty-four years never waned. The record of that wonder can still be found in his essays on birds in this book, just a small harvest from a very rich and plentiful yield. In the eye of a field sparrow, ringed lightly, there is wonder, a wonder equal to creation, waiting. It can be found by anyone who keeps a sharp lookout. To see the eye ring and feel the wonder is a form of devotion, a devotion lived daily by John Burroughs. Open the door to Burroughs's world of birds as you open this book, and begin or continue your acquaintance. And welcome to you. Be sure to pack a good lunch.

JACK KLIGERMAN
Associate Professor of English
Herbert H. Lehman College
City University of New York

NOTES

1. John Burroughs, *The Writings of John Burroughs*, VII, p. 7. References throughout this introduction are to this, the Riverby Edition of his works. Hereafter cited as *Writings*. References are to volume number and page number.

2. Clara Barrus, *The Life and Letters of John Burroughs*, I, p. 274. Hereafter cited as *Life*. References are to volume number and page number.

3. John Burroughs, *The Heart of Burroughs's Journals*, p. 286. Hereafter cited as *Journals*. References are to page number.

4. Ralph Waldo Emerson, *Nature: A Facsimile of the First Edition*, p. 33.

5. Henry James, *Views and Reviews*, p. 217. Originally published in *The Nation*, January 27, 1876.

6. Robert Henry Welker, *Birds and Men: American Birds in Science, Art, Literature and Conservation, 1800-1900*, pp. 85-86.

7. Norman Foerster, *Nature in American Literature*, p. 254.

8. Walt Whitman, *Leaves of Grass*, vv. 662-663.

9. Bashō, *The Narrow Road to the Deep North*, p. 33.

10. Whitman, *Leaves of Grass*, p. 13.

11. Ibid., vv. 36–37.

12. See *John Burroughs: Naturalist* and *John Burroughs' Slabsides*, passim. I would like to thank Mrs. Kelley specifically at this point for kindly talking to me about her grandfather and for some helpful information about the text of his essays.

13. Dallas Lore Sharp, "Fifty Years of John Burroughs," p. 41.

14. Emerson, *Nature*, p. 190. Italics mine.

15. Clara Barrus, *Whitman and Burroughs: Comrades*, p. 88.

16. William D. Howells, review of *Wake-Robin*, p. 254.

17. Bliss Perry, *The Praise of Folly*, pp. 71-72.

A NOTE ON THE BIRDS

Below are the names of birds used by John Burroughs in his essays; each is followed by its modern equivalent as found in Roger Tory Peterson, *A Field Guide to the Birds* (Boston: Houghton Mifflin Company, 1947). Common nineteenth-century bird names can be found in Austin C. Apgar, *Birds of the United States East of the Rocky Mountains* (New York: American Book Company, 1898).

Black and white creeping warbler	Black and white warbler
Bush sparrow	Field sparrow
Buzzard	Turkey vulture
Canada sparrow	Tree sparrow
Cedar-bird	Cedar waxwing
Chewink	Towhee
Chimney swallow	Chimney swift
Common pewee	Wood pewee
Cow blackbird	Cowbird
Crow blackbird	Purple grackle
Ferruginous thrush	Veery
Fish hawk	Osprey
Golden-crowned thrush	Oven-bird
Golden-shafted woodpecker	Flicker
Great-crested flycatcher	Crested flycatcher
Green-crested pewee	Acadian flycatcher
Hairbird	Chipping sparrow
Hen hawk	Red-tailed hawk or other soaring hawk
High-hole	Flicker
Indigo-bird	Indigo bunting
Large-billed water-thrush	Louisiana water-thrush

A NOTE ON THE BIRDS

Maryland yellow-throat	Common yellow throat
Mourning ground warbler	Mourning warbler
New York water-thrush	Northern water-thrush
Orchard starling	Orchard oriole
Partridge	Ruffed grouse
Phoebe-bird	Eastern phoebe
Pine linnet	Pine siskin
Pinnated grouse	Prairie chicken
Red owl	Screech owl (red phase)
Red-shouldered starling	Red-winged blackbird
Rusty grackle	Rusty blackbird
Shore lark	Horned lark
Snowbird	Slate-colored junco
Social sparrow	Chipping sparrow
Solitary vireo	Blue-headed vireo
Turtle-dove	Mourning dove
White-bellied swallow	Tree swallow
Wilson's thrush	Veery
Yellow-bellied woodpecker	Yellow-bellied sapsucker
Yellow redpoll	Palm warbler

WINTER NEIGHBORS

THE country is more of a wilderness, more of a wild solitude, in the winter than in the summer. The wild comes out. The urban, the cultivated, is hidden or negatived. You hardly know a good field from a poor, a meadow from a pasture, a park from a forest. Lines and boundaries are disregarded ; gates and bar-ways are unclosed ; man lets go his hold upon the earth ; title-deeds are deep buried beneath the snow ; the best-kept grounds relapse to a state of nature ; under the pressure of the cold, all the wild creatures become outlaws, and roam abroad beyond their usual haunts. The partridge comes to the orchard for buds ; the rabbit comes to the garden and lawn ; the crows and jays come to the ash-heap and corn-crib, the snow buntings to the stack and to the barnyard ; the sparrows pilfer from the domestic fowls ; the pine grosbeak comes down from the north and shears your maples of their buds ; the fox prowls about your premises at night ; and the red squirrels find your grain in the barn or steal the butternuts from your attic. In fact, winter, like

37

Downy Woodpecker

some great calamity, changes the status of most creatures and sets them adrift. Winter, like poverty, makes us acquainted with strange bedfellows.

For my part, my nearest approach to a strange bedfellow is the little gray rabbit that has taken up her abode under my study floor. As she spends the day here and is out larking at night, she is not much of a bedfellow, after all. It is probable that I disturb her slumbers more than she does mine. I think she is some support to me under there, — a silent, wide-eyed witness and backer; a type of the gentle and harmless in savage nature. She has no sagacity to give me or to lend me, but that soft, nimble foot of hers, and that touch as of cotton wherever she goes, are worthy of emulation. I think I can feel her good-will through the floor, and I hope she can mine. When I have a happy thought, I imagine her ears twitch, especially when I think of the sweet apple I will place by her doorway at night. I wonder if that fox chanced to catch a glimpse of her the other night when he stealthily leaped over the fence near by and walked along between the study and the house? How clearly one could read that it was not a little dog that had passed there! There was something furtive in the track; it shied off away from the house and around it, as if eying it suspiciously; and then it had the caution and deliberation of the fox,— bold, bold, but not too bold; wariness was in every footprint. If it had been a little dog that had chanced to wander that way, when he crossed my path he would have followed it up to the barn and have gone smelling around for a bone; but this sharp, cautious track held straight across all others, keeping five or six rods from the house, up the hill, across the highway toward a neighboring farmstead, with its nose in the air, and its eye and ear alert, so to speak.

A winter neighbor of mine, in whom I am interested, and who perhaps lends me his support after his kind, is a little red owl, whose retreat is in the heart of an old apple-tree just over the fence. Where he keeps himself in spring and summer, I do not know, but late every fall, and at intervals all winter, his hiding-place is discovered by the jays and nuthatches, and proclaimed from the tree-tops for the space of half an hour or so, with all the powers of voice they can command. Four times during one winter they called me out to behold this little ogre feigning sleep in his den, sometimes in one apple-tree, sometimes in another. Whenever I heard their cries, I knew my neighbor was being berated. The birds would take turns at looking in upon him, and uttering their alarm-notes. Every jay within hearing would come to the spot, and at once approach the hole in the trunk or limb, and with a kind of breathless eagerness and excitement take a peep at the owl, and then join the outcry. When I approached they would hastily take a final look, and then withdraw and regard my movements intently. After accustoming my eye to the faint light of the cavity for a few moments, I could usually make out the owl at the bottom feigning sleep. Feigning, I say, because this is what he really did, as I first discovered one day when I cut into his retreat with the axe. The loud blows and the falling chips did not disturb him at all. When I reached in a stick and pulled him over on his side, leaving one of his wings spread out, he made no attempt to recover himself, but lay among the chips and fragments of decayed wood, like a part of themselves. Indeed, it took a sharp eye to distinguish him. Not till I had pulled him forth by one wing, rather rudely, did he abandon his trick of simulated sleep or death. Then, like a detected pickpocket, he was suddenly transformed into another creature. His eyes flew wide open, his talons clutched my finger, his ears were depressed, and every motion and look said, " Hands off, at your peril." Finding this game did not work, he soon began to " play possum " again. I put a cover over my study wood-box and kept him captive for a week. Look in upon him at any time, night or day, and he was apparently wrapped in the profoundest slumber ; but the live mice which I put into his box from time to time found his sleep was easily broken ; there would be a sudden rustle in the box, a faint squeak, and then silence. After a week of captivity I gave him his freedom in the full sunshine : no trouble for him to see which way and where to go.

Just at dusk in the winter nights, I often hear his soft *bur-r-r-r*, very pleasing and bell-like. What a furtive, woody sound it is in the winter stillness, so unlike the harsh scream of the hawk! But all the ways of the owl are ways of softness and duskiness. His wings are shod with silence, his plumage is edged with down.

Another owl neighbor of mine, with whom I pass the time of day more frequently than with the last, lives farther away. I pass his castle every night on my way to the post-office, and in winter, if the hour is late enough, am pretty sure to see him standing in his doorway, surveying the passers-by and the landscape through narrow slits in his eyes. For four successive winters now have I observed him. As the twilight begins to deepen, he rises up out of his cavity in the apple-tree, scarcely faster than the moon rises from behind the hill, and sits in the opening, completely framed by its outlines of gray bark and dead wood, and by his protective coloring virtually invisible to every eye that does not know he is there. Probably my own is the only eye that has ever penetrated his secret, and mine never would have done so had I not chanced on one occasion to see him leave his retreat and make a raid upon a shrike that was impaling a shrew-mouse upon a thorn in a neighboring tree, and which I was watching. Failing to get the mouse, the owl returned swiftly to his cavity, and ever since, while going that way, I have been on the lookout for him. Dozens of teams and foot-passengers pass him late in the day, but he regards them not, nor they him. When I come along and pause to salute him, he opens his eyes a little wider, and, appearing to recognize me, quickly shrinks and fades into the background of his door in a very weird and curious manner. When he is not at his outlook, or when he is, it requires the best powers of the eye to decide the point, as the empty cavity itself is almost an exact image of him. If the whole thing had been carefully studied, it could not have answered its purpose better. The owl stands quite perpendicular, presenting a front of light mottled gray; the eyes are closed to a mere slit, the ear-feathers depressed, the beak buried in the plumage, and the whole attitude is one of silent, motionless waiting and observation. If a mouse should be seen crossing the highway, or scudding over any exposed part of the snowy surface in the twilight, the owl would doubtless swoop down upon it. I think the owl has learned to distinguish me from the rest of the passers-by; at least, when I stop before him, and he sees himself observed, he backs down into his den, as I have said, in a very amusing manner. Whether bluebirds, nuthatches, and chickadees — birds that pass the night in cavities of trees — ever run into the clutches of the dozing owl, I should be glad to know. My impression is, however, that they seek out smaller cavities. An old willow by the roadside blew down one summer, and a decayed branch broke open, revealing a brood of half-fledged owls, and many feathers and quills of bluebirds, orioles, and other songsters, showing plainly enough why all birds fear and berate the owl.

The English house sparrows, which are so rapidly increasing among us, and which must add greatly to the food supply of the owls and other birds of prey, seek to baffle their enemies by roosting in the densest evergreens they can find, in the arbor-vitæ, and in hemlock hedges. Soft-winged as the owl is, he cannot steal in upon such a retreat without giving them warning.

These sparrows are becoming about the most noticeable of my winter neighbors, and a troop of them every morning watch me put out the hens' feed, and soon claim their share. I rather encouraged them in their neighborliness, till one day I discovered the snow under a favorite plum-tree where they most frequently perched covered with the scales of the fruit-buds. On investigating, I found that the tree had been nearly stripped of its buds, — a very unneighborly act on the part of the sparrows, considering, too, all the cracked corn I had scattered for them. So I at once served notice on them that our good understanding was at an end. And a hint is as good as a kick with this bird. The stone I hurled among them, and the one with which I followed them up, may have been taken as a kick; but they were only a hint of the shotgun that stood ready in the corner. The sparrows left in high dudgeon, and were not back again in some days, and were then very shy. No doubt the time is near at hand when we shall have to wage serious war upon these sparrows, as they long have had to do on the continent of Europe. And yet it will be hard to kill the little wretches, the only Old World birds we have. When I take down my gun to shoot them I shall probably remember that the Psalmist said, " I watch, and am as a sparrow alone upon the housetop," and maybe the recollection will cause me to stay my hand. The sparrows have the Old World hardiness and prolificness; they are wise and tenacious of life, and we shall find it by and by no small matter to keep them in check. Our native birds are much different, less prolific, less shrewd, less aggressive and persistent, less quick-witted and able to read the note of danger or hostility, — in short, less sophisticated. Most of our birds are yet essentially wild, that is, little changed by civilization. In winter, especially, they sweep by me and around me in flocks, — the Canada sparrow, the snow bunting, the shore lark, the pine grosbeak, the redpoll, the cedar-bird, — feeding upon frozen apples in the orchard, upon cedar-berries, upon maple-buds, and the berries of the mountain-ash, and the celtis, and upon the seeds of the weeds that rise above the snow in the fields, or upon the hay-seed dropped where the cattle have been foddered in the barnyard or about the distant stack ; but yet taking no heed of man, in no way changing their habits so as to take advantage of his presence in nature. The pine grosbeaks will come in numbers upon your porch to get the black drupes of the honeysuckle or the woodbine, or within reach of your windows to get the berries of the mountain-ash, but they know you not ; they look at you as innocently and unconcernedly as at a bear or moose in their native north, and your house is no more to them than a ledge of rocks.

The only ones of my winter neighbors that actually rap at my door are the nuthatches and woodpeckers, and these do not know that it is my door. My retreat is covered with the bark of young chestnut-trees, and the birds, I suspect, mistake it for a huge stump that ought to hold fat grubs (there is not even a book-worm inside of it), and their loud rapping often makes me think I have a caller indeed. I place fragments of hickory-nuts in the interstices of the bark, and thus attract the nuthatches ; a bone upon my window-sill attracts both nuthatches and the downy woodpecker. They peep in curiously through the window upon me, pecking away at my bone, too often a very poor one. A bone nailed to a tree a few feet in front of the window attracts crows as well as lesser birds. Even the slate-colored snowbird, a seed-eater, comes and nibbles it occasionally.

The bird that seems to consider he has the best right to the bone both upon the tree and upon the sill is the downy woodpecker, my favorite neighbor among the winter birds, to whom I will mainly devote the remainder of this chapter. His retreat is but a few paces from my own, in the decayed limb of an apple-tree, which he excavated several autumns ago. I say "he" because the red plume on the top of his head proclaims the sex. It seems not to be generally known to our writers upon ornithology that certain of our woodpeckers — probably all the winter residents — each fall excavate a limb or the trunk of a tree in which to pass the winter, and that the cavity is abandoned in the spring, probably for a new one in which nidification takes place. So far as I have observed, these cavities are drilled out only by the males. Where the females take up their quarters I am not so well informed, though I suspect that they use the abandoned holes of the males of the previous year.

The particular woodpecker to which I refer drilled his first hole in my apple-tree one fall four or five years ago. This he occupied till the following spring, when he abandoned it. The next fall he began a hole in an adjoining limb, later than before, and when it was about half completed a female took possession of his old quarters. I am sorry to say that this seemed to enrage the male very much, and he persecuted the poor bird whenever she appeared upon the scene. He would fly at her spitefully and drive her off. One chilly November morning, as I passed under the tree, I heard the hammer of the little architect in his cavity, and at the same time saw the persecuted female sitting at the entrance of the other hole as if she would fain come out. She was actually shivering, probably from both fear and cold. I understood the situation at a glance; the bird was afraid to come forth and brave the anger of the male. Not till I had rapped smartly upon the limb with my stick did she come out and attempt to escape; but she had not gone ten feet from the tree before the male was in hot pursuit, and in a few moments had driven her back to the same tree, where she tried to avoid him among the branches. A few days after, he rid himself of his unwelcome neighbor in the following ingenious manner: he fairly scuttled the other cavity; he drilled a hole into the bottom of it that let in the light and the cold, and I saw the female there no more. I did not see him in the act of rendering this tenement uninhabitable; but one morning, behold it was punctured at the bottom, and the circumstances all seemed to point to him as the author of it. There is probably no gallantry among the birds except at the mating season. I have frequently seen the male woodpecker drive the female away from the bone upon the tree. When she hopped around to the other end and timidly nibbled it, he would presently dart spitefully at her. She would then take up her position in his rear and wait till he had finished his meal. The position of the female among the birds is very much the same as that of women among savage tribes. Most of the drudgery of life falls upon her, and the leavings of the males are often her lot.

My bird is a genuine little savage, doubtless, but I value him as a neighbor. It is a satisfaction during the cold or stormy winter nights to know he is warm and cozy there in his retreat. When the day is bad and unfit to be abroad in, he is there too. When I wish to know if he is at home, I go and rap upon his tree, and, if he is not too lazy or indifferent, after some delay he shows his head in his round doorway about ten feet above, and looks down inquiringly upon me, — sometimes latterly I think half resentfully, as much as to say, " I would thank you not to disturb me so often." After sundown, he will not put his head out any more when I call, but as I step away I can get a glimpse of him inside looking cold and reserved. He is a late riser, especially if it is a cold or disagreeable morning, in this respect being like the barn fowls; it is sometimes near nine o'clock before I see him leave his tree. On the other hand, he comes home early, being in, if the day is unpleasant, by four P. M. He lives all alone; in this respect I do not commend his example. Where his mate is, I should like to know.

I have discovered several other woodpeckers in adjoining orchards, each of which has a like home, and leads a like solitary life. One of them has excavated a dry limb within easy reach of my hand, doing the work also in September. But the choice of tree was not a good one; the limb was too much decayed, and the workman had made the cavity too large; a chip had come out, making a hole in the outer wall. Then he went a few inches down the limb and began again, and excavated a large, commodious chamber, but had again come too near the surface; scarcely more than the bark protected him in one place, and the limb was very much weakened. Then he made another attempt still farther down the limb, and drilled in an inch or two, but seemed to change his mind; the work stopped, and I concluded the bird had wisely abandoned the tree. Passing there one cold, rainy November day, I thrust in my two fingers and was surprised to feel something soft and warm: as I drew away my hand the bird came out, apparently no more surprised than I was. It had decided, then, to make its home in the old limb; a decision it had occasion to regret, for not long after, on a stormy night, the branch gave way and fell to the ground: —

> " When the bough breaks the cradle will fall,
> And down will come baby, cradle and all."

Such a cavity makes a snug, warm home, and when the entrance is on the under side of the limb, as is usual, the wind and snow cannot reach the occupant. Late in December, while crossing a high, wooded mountain, lured by the music of fox-hounds, I discovered fresh yellow chips strewing the new-fallen snow, and at once thought of my woodpeckers. On looking around I saw where one had been at work excavating a lodge in a small yellow birch. The orifice was about fifteen feet from the ground, and appeared as round as if struck with a compass. It was on the east side of the tree, so as to avoid the prevailing west and northwest winds. As it was nearly two inches in diameter, it could not have been the work of the downy, but must have been that of the hairy, or else the yellow-bellied woodpecker. His home had probably been wrecked by some violent wind, and he was thus providing himself another. In digging out these retreats the woodpeckers prefer a dry, brittle trunk, not too soft. They go in horizontally to the centre and then turn downward, enlarging the tunnel as they go, till when finished it is the shape of a long, deep pear.

Another trait our woodpeckers have that endears them to me, and that has never been pointedly noticed by our ornithologists, is their habit of drumming in the spring. They are songless birds, and yet all are musicians; they make the dry limbs eloquent of the coming change. Did you think that loud, sonorous hammering which proceeded from the orchard or from the near woods on that still March or April morning was only some bird getting its breakfast? It is downy, but he is not rapping at the door of a grub; he is rapping at the door of spring, and the dry limb thrills beneath the ardor of his blows. Or, later in the season, in the dense forest or by some remote mountain lake, does that measured rhythmic beat that breaks upon the silence, first three strokes following each other rapidly, succeeded by two louder ones with longer intervals between them, and that has an effect upon the alert ear as if the solitude itself had at last found a voice, — does that suggest anything less than a deliberate musical performance? In fact, our woodpeckers are just as characteristically drummers as is the ruffed grouse, and they have their particular limbs and stubs to which they resort for that purpose. Their need of expression is apparently just as great as that of the song-birds, and it is not surprising that they should have found out that there is music in a dry, seasoned limb which can be evoked beneath their beaks.

A few seasons ago, a downy woodpecker, probably the individual one who is now my winter neighbor, began to drum early in March in a partly decayed apple-tree that stands in the edge of a narrow strip of woodland near me. When the morning was still and mild I would often hear him through my window before I was up, or by half-past six o'clock, and he would keep it up pretty briskly till nine or ten o'clock, in this respect resembling the grouse, which do most of their drumming in the forenoon. His drum was the stub of a dry limb about the size of one's wrist. The heart was decayed and gone, but the outer shell was hard and resonant. The bird would keep his position there for an hour at a time. Between his drummings he would preen his plumage and listen as if for the response of the female, or for the drum of some rival. How swift his head would go when he was delivering his blows upon the limb! His beak wore the surface perceptibly. When he wished to change the key, which was quite often, he would shift his position an inch or two to a knot which gave out a higher, shriller note. When I climbed up to examine his drum, he was much disturbed. I did not know he was in the vicinity, but it seems he saw me from a near tree, and came in haste to the neighboring branches, and with spread plumage and a sharp note demanded plainly enough what my business was with his drum. I was invading his privacy, desecrating his shrine, and the bird was much put out. After some weeks the female appeared; he had literally drummed up a mate; his urgent and oft-repeated advertisement was answered. Still the drumming did not cease, but was quite as fervent as before. If a mate could be won by drumming, she could be kept and entertained by more drumming; courtship should not end with marriage. If the bird felt musical before, of course he felt much more so now. Besides that, the gentle deities needed propitiating in behalf of the nest and young as well as in behalf of the mate. After a time a second female came, when there was war between the two. I did not see them come to blows, but I saw one female pursuing the other about the place, and giving her no rest for several days. She was evidently trying to run her out of the neighborhood. Now and then, she, too, would drum briefly, as if sending a triumphant message to her mate.

The woodpeckers do not each have a particular dry limb to which they resort at all times to drum, like the one I have described. The woods are full of suitable branches, and they drum more or less here and there as they are in quest of food; yet I am convinced each one has its favorite spot, like the grouse, to which it resorts especially in the morning. The sugar-maker in the maple-woods may notice that this sound proceeds from the same tree or trees about his camp with great regularity. A woodpecker in my vicinity has drummed for two seasons on a telegraph pole, and he makes the wires and glass insulators ring. Another drums on a thin board on the end of a long grape-arbor, and on still mornings can be heard a long distance.

A friend of mine in a Southern city tells me of a red-headed woodpecker that drums upon a lightning-rod on his neighbor's house. Nearly every clear, still morning at certain seasons, he says, this musical rapping may be heard. "He alternates his tapping with his stridulous call, and the effect on a cool, autumn-like morning is very pleasing."

The high-hole appears to drum more promiscuously than does downy. He utters his long, loud spring call, *whick — whick — whick — whick*, and then begins to rap with his beak upon his perch before the last note has reached your ear. I have seen him drum sitting upon the ridge of the barn. The log-cock, or pileated woodpecker, the largest and wildest of our Northern species, I never have heard drum. His blows should wake the echoes.

When the woodpecker is searching for food, or laying siege to some hidden grub, the sound of his hammer is dead or muffled, and is heard but a few yards. It is only upon dry, seasoned timber, freed of its bark, that he beats his reveille to spring and wooes his mate.

Wilson was evidently familiar with this vernal drumming of the woodpeckers, but quite misinterprets it. Speaking of the red-bellied species, he says : " It rattles like the rest of the tribe on the dead limbs, and with such violence as to be heard in still weather more than half a mile off ; and listens to hear the insect it has alarmed." He listens rather to hear the drum of his rival, or the brief and coy response of the female; for there are no insects in these dry limbs.

On one occasion I saw downy at his drum when a female flew quickly through the tree and alighted a few yards beyond him. He paused instantly, and kept his place apparently without moving a muscle. The female, I took it, had answered his advertisement. She flitted about from limb to limb (the female may be known by the absence of the crimson spot on the back of the head), apparently full of business of her own, and now and then would drum in a shy, tentative manner. The male watched her a few moments, and, convinced perhaps that she meant business, struck up his liveliest tune, then listened for her response. As it came back timidly but promptly, he left his perch and sought a nearer acquaintance with the prudent female. Whether or not a match grew out of this little flirtation I cannot say.

The downy woodpeckers are sometimes accused of injuring the apple and other fruit trees, but the depredator is probably the larger and rarer yellow-bellied species. One autumn I caught one of these fellows in the act of sinking long rows of his little wells in the limb of an apple-tree. There were series of rings of them, one above another, quite around the stem, some of them the third of an inch across. They are evidently made to get at the tender, juicy bark, or cambium layer, next to the hard wood of the tree. The health and vitality of the branch are so seriously impaired by them that it often dies.

In the following winter the same bird (probably) tapped a maple-tree in front of my window in fifty-six places; and when the day was sunny, and the sap oozed out, he spent most of his time there. He knew the good sap-days, and was on hand promptly for his tipple; cold and cloudy days he did not appear. He knew which side of the tree to tap, too, and avoided the sunless northern exposure. When one series of well-holes failed to supply him, he would sink another, drilling through the bark with great ease and quickness. Then, when the day was warm, and the sap ran freely, he would have a regular sugar-maple debauch, sitting there by his wells hour after hour, and as fast as they became filled sipping out the sap. This he did in a gentle, caressing manner that was very suggestive. He made a row of wells near the foot of the tree, and other rows higher up, and he would hop up and down the trunk as these became filled. He would hop down the tree backward with the utmost ease, throwing his tail outward and his head inward at each hop. When the wells would freeze up or his thirst become slaked, he would ruffle his feathers, draw himself together, and sit and doze in the sun on the side of the tree. He passed the night in a hole in an apple-tree not far off. He was evidently a young bird, not yet having the plumage of the mature male or female, and yet he knew which tree to tap and where to tap it. I saw where he had bored several maples in the vicinity, but no oaks or chestnuts. I nailed up a fat bone near his sap-works: the downy woodpecker came there several times a day to dine; the nuthatch came, and even the snowbird took a taste occasionally; but this sapsucker never touched it; the sweet of the tree sufficed for him. This woodpecker does not breed or abound in my vicinity; only stray specimens are now and then to be met with in the colder months. As spring approached, the one I refer to took his departure.

I must bring my account of my neighbor in the tree down to the latest date; so after the lapse of a year I add the following notes. The last day of February was bright and spring-like. I heard the first sparrow sing that morning and the first screaming of the circling hawks, and about seven o'clock the first drumming of my little friend. His first notes were uncertain and at long intervals, but by and by he warmed up and beat a lively tattoo. As the season advanced he ceased to lodge in his old quarters. I would rap and find nobody at home. Was he out on a lark, I said, the spring fever working in his blood? After a time his drumming grew less frequent, and finally, in the middle of April, ceased entirely. Had some accident befallen him, or had he wandered away to fresh fields, following some siren of his species? Probably the latter. Another bird that I had under observation also left his winter-quarters in the spring. This, then, appears to be the usual custom. The wrens and the nuthatches and chickadees succeed to these abandoned cavities, and often have amusing disputes over them. The nuthatches frequently pass the night in them, and the wrens and chickadees nest in them. I have further observed that in excavating a cavity for a nest the downy woodpecker makes the entrance smaller than when he is excavating his winter-quarters. This is doubtless for the greater safety of the young birds.

The next fall the downy excavated another limb in the old apple-tree, but had not got his retreat quite finished when the large hairy woodpecker appeared upon the scene. I heard his loud *click*, *click*, early one frosty November morning. There was something impatient and angry in the tone that arrested my attention. I saw the bird fly to the tree where downy had been at work, and fall with great violence upon the entrance to his cavity. The bark and the chips flew beneath his vigorous' blows, and, before I fairly woke up to what he was doing, he had completely demolished the neat, round doorway of downy. He had made a large, ragged opening, large enough for himself to enter. I drove him away and my favorite came back, but only to survey the ruins of his castle for a moment and then go away. He lingered about for a day or two and then disappeared. The big hairy usurper passed a night in the cavity; but on being hustled out of it the next night by me, he also left, but not till he had demolished the entrance to a cavity in a neighboring tree where downy and his mate had reared their brood that summer, and where I had hoped the female would pass the winter.

THE BLUEBIRD

WHEN Nature made the bluebird she wished to propitiate both the sky and the earth, so she gave him the color of the one on his back and the hue of the other on his breast, and ordained that his appearance in spring should denote that the strife and war between these two elements was at an end. He is the peace-harbinger; in him the celestial and terrestrial strike hands and are fast friends. He means the furrow and he means the warmth; he means all the soft, wooing influences of the spring on the one hand, and the retreating footsteps of winter on the other.

It is sure to be a bright March morning when you first hear his note; and it is as if the milder influences up above had found a voice and let a word fall upon your ear, so tender is it and so prophetic, a hope tinged with a regret.

"*Bermuda! Bermuda! Bermuda!*" he seems to say, as if both invoking and lamenting, and, behold! Bermuda follows close, though the little pilgrim may be only repeating the tradition of his race, himself having come only from Florida, the

Carolinas, or even from Virginia, where he has found his Bermuda on some broad sunny hillside thickly studded with cedars and persimmon-trees.

In New York and in New England the sap starts up in the sugar maple the very day the bluebird arrives, and sugar-making begins forthwith. The bird is generally a mere disembodied voice; a rumor in the air for two or three days before it takes' visible shape before you. The males are the pioneers, and come several days in advance of the females. By the time both are here and the pairs have begun to prospect for a place to nest, sugar-making is over, the last vestige of snow has disappeared, and the plow is brightening its mould-board in the new furrow.

The bluebird enjoys the preëminence of being the first bit of color that cheers our northern landscape. The other birds that arrive about the same time — the sparrow, the robin, the phœbe-bird — are clad in neutral tints, gray, brown, or russet; but the bluebird brings one of the primary hues and the divinest of them all.

This bird also has the distinction of answering very nearly to the robin redbreast of English memory, and was by the early settlers of New England christened the blue robin.

It is a size or two larger, and the ruddy hue of its breast does not verge so nearly on an orange, but the manners and habits of the two birds are very

Bluebird

much alike. Our bird has the softer voice, but the English redbreast is much the more skilled musician. He has indeed a fine, animated warble, heard nearly the year through about English gardens and along the old hedge-rows, that is quite beyond the compass of our bird's instrument. On the other hand, our bird is associated with the spring as the British species cannot be, being a winter resident also, while the brighter sun and sky of the New World have given him a coat that far surpasses that of his transatlantic cousin.

It is worthy of remark that among British birds there is no *blue* bird. The cerulean tint seems much rarer among the feathered tribes there than here. On this continent there are at least three species of the common bluebird, while in all our woods there is the blue jay and the indigo-bird, — the latter so intensely blue as to fully justify its name. There is also the blue grosbeak, not much behind the indigo-bird in intensity of color; and among our warblers the blue tint is very common.

It is interesting to know that the bluebird is not confined to any one section of the country; and that when one goes West he will still have this favorite with him, though a little changed in voice and color, just enough to give variety without marring the identity.

The Western bluebird is considered a distinct species, and is perhaps a little more brilliant and showy than its Eastern brother; and Nuttall thinks its song is more varied, sweet, and tender. Its color approaches to ultramarine, while it has a sash of chestnut-red across its shoulders, — all the effects, I suspect, of that wonderful air and sky of California, and of those great Western plains; or, if one goes a little higher up into the mountainous regions of the West, he finds the Arctic bluebird, the ruddy brown on the breast changed to greenish blue, and the wings longer and more pointed; in other respects not differing much from our species.

The bluebird usually builds its nest in a hole in a stump or stub, or in an old cavity excavated by a woodpecker, when such can be had; but its first impulse seems to be to start in the world in much more style, and the happy pair make a great show of house-hunting about the farm buildings, now half persuaded to appropriate a dove-cote, then discussing in a lively manner a last year's swallow's nest, or proclaiming with much flourish and flutter that they have taken the wren's house, or the tenement of the purple martin; till finally nature becomes too urgent, when all this pretty make-believe ceases, and most of them settle back upon the old family stumps and knotholes in remote fields, and go to work in earnest.

In such situations the female is easily captured by approaching very stealthily and covering the entrance to the nest. The bird seldom makes any effort to escape, seeing how hopeless the case is, and keeps her place on the nest till she feels your hand closing around her. I have looked down into the cavity and seen the poor thing palpitating with fear and looking up with distended eyes, but never moving till I had withdrawn a few paces; then she rushes out with a cry that brings the male on the scene in a hurry. He warbles and lifts his wings beseechingly, but shows no anger or disposition to scold and complain like most birds. Indeed, this bird seems incapable of uttering a harsh note, or of doing a spiteful, ill-tempered thing.

The ground-builders all have some art or device to decoy one away from the nest, affecting lameness, a crippled wing, or a broken back, promising an easy capture if pursued. The tree-builders depend upon concealing the nest or placing it beyond reach. But the bluebird has no art either way, and its nest is easily found.

About the only enemies the sitting bird or the nest is in danger of are snakes and squirrels. I knew of a farm-boy who was in the habit of putting his hand down into a bluebird's nest and taking out the old bird whenever he came that way. One day he put his hand in, and, feeling something peculiar, withdrew it hastily, when it was instantly followed by the head and neck of an enormous black snake. The boy took to his heels and the snake gave chase.

pressing him close till a plowman near by came to the rescue with his ox-whip.

There never was a happier or more devoted husband than the male bluebird is. But among nearly all our familiar birds the serious cares of life seem to devolve almost entirely upon the female. The male is hilarious and demonstrative, the female serious and anxious about her charge. The male is the attendant of the female, following her wherever she goes. He never leads, never directs, but only seconds and applauds. If his life is all poetry and romance, hers is all business and prose. She has no pleasure but her duty, and no duty but to look after her nest and brood. She shows no affection for the male, no pleasure in his society; she only tolerates him as a necessary evil, and, if he is killed, goes in quest of another in the most business-like manner, as you would go for the plumber or the glazier. In most cases the male is the ornamental partner in the firm, and contributes little of the working capital. There seems to be more equality of the sexes among the woodpeckers, wrens, and swallows; while the contrast is greatest, perhaps, in the bobolink family, where the courting is done in the Arab fashion, the female fleeing with all her speed and the male pursuing with equal precipitation; and were it not for the broods of young birds that appear, it would be hard to believe that the intercourse ever ripened into anything more intimate.

With the bluebirds the male is useful as well as ornamental. He is the gay champion and escort of the female at all times, and while she is sitting he feeds her regularly. It is very pretty to watch them building their nest. The male is very active in hunting out a place and exploring the boxes and cavities, but seems to have no choice in the matter and is anxious only to please and encourage his mate, who has the practical turn and knows what will do and what will not. After she has suited herself he applauds her immensely, and away the two go in quest of material for the nest, the male acting as guard and flying above and in advance of the female. She brings all the material and does all the work of building, he looking on and encouraging her with gesture and song. He acts also as inspector of her work, but I fear is a very partial one. She enters the nest with her bit of dry grass or straw, and, having adjusted it to her notion, withdraws and waits near by while he goes in and looks it over. On coming out he exclaims very plainly, " *Excellent ! excellent !* " and away the two go again for more material.

The bluebirds, when they build about the farm buildings, sometimes come in conflict with the swallows. The past season I knew a pair to take forcible possession of the domicile of a pair of the latter, — the cliff species that now stick their nests under the eaves of the barn. The bluebirds had been broken up in a little bird-house near by, by the rats or perhaps a weasel, and being no doubt in a bad humor, and the season being well advanced, they made forcible entrance into the adobe tenement of their neighbors, and held possession of it for some days, but I believe finally withdrew, rather than live amid such a squeaky, noisy colony. I have heard that these swallows, when ejected from their homes in that way by the phœbe-bird, have been known to fall to and mason up the entrance to the nest while their enemy was inside of it, thus having a revenge as complete and cruel as anything in human annals.

The bluebirds and the house wrens more frequently come into collision. A few years ago I put up a little bird-house in the back end of my garden for the accommodation of the wrens, and every season a pair have taken up their abode there. One spring a pair of bluebirds looked into the tenement and lingered about several days, leading me to hope that they would conclude to occupy it. But they finally went away, and later in the season the wrens appeared, and, after a little coquetting, were regularly installed in their old quarters, and were as happy as only wrens can be.

One of our younger poets, Myron Benton, saw a little bird

" Ruffled with whirlwind of his ecstasies,"

which must have been the wren, as I know of no other bird that so throbs and palpitates with music as this little vagabond. And the pair I speak of seemed exceptionably happy, and the male had a small tornado of song in his crop that kept him "ruffled" every moment in the day. But before their honeymoon was over the bluebirds returned. I knew something was wrong before I was up in the morning. Instead of that voluble and gushing song outside the window, I heard the wrens scolding and crying at a fearful rate, and on going out saw the bluebirds in possession of the box. The poor wrens were in despair; they wrung their hands and tore their hair, after the wren fashion, but chiefly did they rattle out their disgust and wrath at the intruders. I have no doubt that, if it could have been interpreted, it would have proven the rankest and most voluble Billingsgate ever uttered. For the wren is saucy, and he has a tongue in his head that can outwag any other tongue known to me.

The bluebirds said nothing, but the male kept an eye on Mr. Wren; and, when he came too near, gave chase, driving him to cover under the fence, or under a rubbish-heap or other object, where the wren would scold and rattle away, while his pursuer sat on the fence or the pea-brush waiting for him to reappear.

Days passed, and the usurpers prospered and the outcasts were wretched; but the latter lingered

about, watching and abusing their enemies, and
hoping, no doubt, that things would take a turn,
as they presently did. The outraged wrens were
fully avenged. The mother bluebird had laid her
full complement of eggs and was beginning to set,
when one day, as her mate was perched above her
on the barn, along came a boy with one of those
wicked elastic slings and cut him down with a pebble. There he lay like a bit of sky fallen upon the
grass. The widowed bird seemed to understand
what had happened, and without much ado disappeared next day in quest of another mate. How
she contrived to make her wants known, without
trumpeting them about, I am unable to say. But I
presume the birds have a way of advertising that
answers the purpose well. Maybe she trusted to
luck to fall in with some stray bachelor or bereaved
male who would undertake to console a widow of
one day's standing. I will say, in passing, that
there are no bachelors from choice among the birds;
they are all rejected suitors, while old maids are
entirely unknown. There is a Jack to every Jill; and
some to boot.

The males, being more exposed by their song and
plumage, and by being the pioneers in migrating,
seem to be slightly in excess lest the supply fall
short, and hence it sometimes happens that a few
are bachelors perforce; there are not females enough
to go around, but before the season is over there are

sure to be some vacancies in the marital ranks, which they are called on to fill.

In the mean time the wrens were beside themselves with delight; they fairly screamed with joy. If the male was before "ruffled with whirlwind of his ecstasies," he was now in danger of being rent asunder. He inflated his throat and caroled as wren never caroled before. And the female, too, how she cackled and darted about! How busy they both were! Rushing into the nest, they hustled those eggs out in less than a minute, wren time. They carried in new material, and by the third day were fairly installed again in their old quarters; but on the third day, so rapidly are these little dramas played, the female bluebird reappeared with another mate. Ah! how the wren stock went down then! What dismay and despair filled again those little breasts! It was pitiful. They did not scold as before, but after a day or two withdrew from the garden, dumb with grief, and gave up the struggle.

The bluebird, finding her eggs gone and her nest changed, seemed suddenly seized with alarm and shunned the box; or else, finding she had less need for another husband than she thought, repented her rashness and wanted to dissolve the compact. But the happy bridegroom would not take the hint, and exerted all his eloquence to comfort and reassure her. He was fresh and fond, and until this bereaved female found him I am sure his suit had not prospered that season. He thought the box just the thing, and that there was no need of alarm, and spent days in trying to persuade the female back. Seeing he could not be a stepfather to a family, he was quite willing to assume a nearer relation. He hovered about the box, he went in and out, he called, he warbled, he entreated; the female would respond occasionally and come and alight near, and even peep into the nest, but would not enter it, and quickly flew away again. Her mate would reluctantly follow, but he was soon back, uttering the most confident and cheering calls. If she did not come he would perch above the nest and sound his loudest notes over and over again, looking in the direction of his mate and beckoning with every motion. But she responded less and less frequently. Some days I would see him only, but finally he gave it up; the pair disappeared, and the box remained deserted the rest of the summer.

1867.

Sapsucker

SPRING JOTTINGS

FOR ten or more years past I have been in the habit of jotting down, among other things in my note-book, observations upon the seasons as they passed, — the complexion of the day, the aspects of nature, the arrival of the birds, the opening of the flowers, or any characteristic feature of the passing moment or hour which the great open-air panorama presented. Some of these notes and observations touching the opening and the progress of the spring season follow herewith.

I need hardly say they are off-hand and informal; what they have to recommend them to the general reader is mainly their fidelity to actual fact. The sun always crosses the line on time, but the seasons which he makes are by no means so punctual; they loiter or they hasten, and the spring tokens are three or four weeks earlier or later some seasons than others. The ice often breaks up on the river early in March, but I have crossed upon it as late as the 10th of April. My journal presents many samples of both early and late springs.

But before I give these extracts, let me say a word

or two in favor of the habit of keeping a journal of one's thoughts and days. To a countryman, especially of a meditative turn, who likes to preserve the flavor of the passing moment, or to a person of leisure anywhere, who wants to make the most of life, a journal will be found a great help. It is a sort of deposit account wherein one saves up bits and fragments of his life that would otherwise be lost to him.

What seemed so insignificant in the passing, or as it lay in embryo in his mind, becomes a valuable part of his experiences when it is fully unfolded and recorded in black and white. The process of writing develops it; the bud becomes the leaf or flower; the one is disentangled from the many and takes definite form and hue. I remember that Thoreau says in a letter to a friend, after his return from a climb to the top of Monadnock, that it is not till he gets home that he really goes over the mountain; that is, I suppose, sees what the climb meant to him when he comes to write an account of it to his friend. Every one's experience is probably much the same; when we try to tell what we saw and felt, even to our journals, we discover more and deeper meanings in things than we had suspected.

The pleasure and value of every walk or journey we take may be doubled to us by carefully noting down the impressions it makes upon us. How much of the flavor of Maine birch I should have missed had I not compelled that vague, unconscious being within me, who absorbs so much and says so little, to unbosom himself at the point of the pen! It was not till after I got home that I really went to Maine, or to the Adirondacks, or to Canada. Out of the chaotic and nebulous impressions which these expeditions gave me, I evolved the real experience. There is hardly anything that does not become much more in the telling than in the thinking or in the feeling.

I see the fishermen floating up and down the river above their nets, which are suspended far out of sight in the water beneath them. They do not know what fish they have got, if any, till after a while they lift the nets up and examine them. In all of us there is a region of subconsciousness above which our ostensible lives go forward, and in which much comes to us, or is slowly developed, of which we are quite ignorant until we lift up our nets and inspect them.

Then the charm and significance of a day are so subtle and fleeting! Before we know it, it is gone past all recovery. I find that each spring, that each summer and fall and winter of my life, has a hue and quality of its own, given by some prevailing mood, a train of thought, an event, an experience, — a color or quality of which I am quite unconscious at the time, being too near to it, and too completely enveloped by it. But afterward some mood or circumstance, an odor, or fragment of a tune, brings it back as by a flash; for one brief second the adamantine door of the past swings open and gives me a glimpse of my former life. One's journal, dashed off without any secondary motive, may often preserve and renew the past for him in this way.

These leaves from my own journal are not very good samples of this sort of thing, but they preserve for me the image of many a day which memory alone could never have kept.

March 3, 1879. The sun is getting strong, but winter still holds his own. No hint of spring in the earth or air. No sparrow or sparrow song yet. But on the 5th there was a hint of spring. The day warm and the snow melting. The first bluebird note this morning. How sweetly it dropped down from the blue overhead!

March 10. A real spring day at last, and a rouser! Thermometer between fifty and sixty degrees in the coolest spot; bees very lively about the hive, and working on the sawdust in the wood-yard; how they dig and wallow in the woody meal, apparently squeezing it, as if forcing it to yield up something to them! Here they get their first substitute for pollen. The sawdust of hickory and maple is preferred. The inner milky substance between the bark and the wood, called the cambium layer, is probably the source of their supplies.

In the growing tree it is in this layer or secretion

that the vital processes are the most active and potent. It has been found by experiment that this tender, milky substance is capable of exerting a very great force; a growing tree exerts a lifting and pushing force of more than thirty pounds to the square inch, and the force is thought to reside in the soft, fragile cells that make up the cambium layer. It is like the strength of Samson residing in his hair. Saw one bee enter the hive with pollen on his back, which he must have got from some open greenhouse; or had he found the skunk cabbage in bloom ahead of me?

The bluebirds! It seemed as if they must have been waiting somewhere close by for the first warm day, like actors behind the scenes, for they were here in numbers early in the morning; they rushed upon the stage very promptly when their parts were called. No robins yet. Sap runs, but not briskly. It is too warm and still; it wants a brisk day for sap, with a certain sharpness in the air, a certain crispness and tension.

March 12. A change to more crispness and coolness, but a delicious spring morning. Hundreds of snowbirds with a sprinkling of song and Canada sparrows are all about the house, chirping and lisping and chattering in a very animated manner. The air is full of bird voices; through this maze of fine sounds comes the strong note and warble of the robin, and the soft call of the bluebird. A few days ago, not a bird, not a sound; everything rigid and severe; then in a day the barriers of winter give way, and spring comes like an inundation. In a twinkling all is changed.

Under date of February 27, 1881, I find this note: "Warm; saw the male bluebird warbling and calling cheerily. The male bluebird spreads his tail as he flits about at this season, in a way to make him look very gay and dressy. It adds to his expression considerably, and makes him look alert and beau-like, and every inch a male. The grass is green under the snow, and has grown perceptibly. The warmth of the air seems to go readily through a covering of ice and snow. Note how quickly the ice lets go of the door-stones, though completely covered, when the day becomes warm."

The farmers say a deep snow draws the frost out of the ground. It is certain that the frost goes out when the ground is deeply covered for some time, though it is of course the warmth rising up from the depths of the ground that does it. A winter of deep snows is apt to prove fatal to the peach buds. The frost leaves the ground, the soil often becomes so warm that angle-worms rise to near the surface, the sap in the trees probably stirs a little; then there comes a cold wave, the mercury goes down to ten or fifteen below zero, and the peach buds are killed. It is not the cold alone that does it; it is the warmth at one end and the extreme cold at the other. When the snow is removed so that the frost can get at the roots also, peach buds will stand fourteen or fifteen degrees below zero.

March 7, 1881. A perfect spring day at last, — still, warm, and without a cloud. Tapped two trees; the sap runs, the snow runs, everything runs. Bluebirds the only birds yet. Thermometer forty-two degrees in the shade. A perfect sap day. A perfect sap day is a crystalline day; the night must have a keen edge of frost, and the day a keen edge of air and sun, with wind north or northwest. The least film, the least breath from the south, the least suggestion of growth, and the day is marred as a sap day. Maple sap is maple frost melted by the sun. (9 P. M.) A soft, large-starred night; the moon in her second quarter; perfectly still and freezing; Venus throbbing low in the west. A crystalline night.

March 21, 1884. The top of a high barometric wave, a day like a crest, lifted up, sightly, sparkling. A cold snap without storm issuing in this clear, dazzling, sharp, northern day. How light, as if illuminated by more than the sun; the sky is full of light; light seems to be streaming up all around the horizon. The leafless trees make no shadows; the woods are flooded with light; everything shines; a day large and imposing, breathing strong masculine breaths out of the north; a day without a speck or film, winnowed through and through, all the windows and doors of the sky open. Day of crumpled rivers and lakes, of crested waves, of bellying sails, high-domed and lustrous day. The only typical March day of the bright heroic sort we have yet had.

March 24, 1884. Damp, still morning, much fog on the river. All the branches and twigs of the trees strung with drops of water. The grass and weeds beaded with fog drops. Two lines of ducks go up the river, one a few feet beneath the other. On second glance the under line proves to be the reflection of the other in the still water. As the ducks cross a large field of ice, the lower line is suddenly blotted out, as if the birds had dived beneath the ice. A train of cars across the river, — the train sunk beneath a solid stratum of fog, its plume of smoke and vapor unrolling above it and slanting away in the distance; a liquid morning; the turf buzzes as you walk over it.

Skunk cabbage on Saturday the 22d, probably in bloom several days. This plant always gets ahead of me. It seems to come up like a mushroom in a single night. Water newts just out, and probably piping before the frogs, though not certain about this.

March 25. One of the rare days that go before a storm; the flower of a series of days increasingly fair. To-morrow, probably, the flower falls, and days of rain and cold prepare the way for another fair day or days. The barometer must be high to-day; the birds fly high. I feed my bees on a rock, and sit long and watch them covering the combs, and rejoice in the multitudinous humming. The river is a great mirror dotted here and there by small cakes of ice. The first sloop comes lazily on up the flood tide, like the first butterfly of spring; the little steamer, our river omnibus, makes her first trip, and wakes the echoes with her salutatory whistle, her flags dancing in the sun.

April 1. Welcome to April, my natal month; the month of the swelling buds, the springing grass, the first nests, the first plantings, the first flowers, and, last but not least, the first shad! The door of the seasons first stands ajar this month, and gives us a peep beyond. The month in which to begin the world, in which to begin your house, in which to begin your courtship, in which to enter upon any new enterprise. The bees usually get their first pollen this month and their first honey. All hibernating creatures are out before April is past. The coon, the chipmunk, the bear, the turtles, the frogs, the snakes, come forth beneath April skies.

April 8. A day of great brightness and clearness, — a crystalline April day that precedes snow. In this sharp crisp air the flakes are forming. As in a warm streaming south wind one can almost smell the swelling buds, so a wind from the opposite quarter at this season as often suggests the crystalline snow. I go up in the sugar bush [this was up among the Catskills], and linger for an hour among the old trees. The air is still, and has the property of being "hollow," as the farmers say; that is, it is heavy, motionless, and transmits sounds well. Every warble of a bluebird or robin, or caw of crow, or bark of dog, or bleat of sheep, or cackle of geese, or call of boy or man, within the landscape, comes distinctly to the ear. The smoke from the chimney goes straight up.

I walk through the bare fields; the shore larks run or flit before me; I hear their shuffling, gurgling, lisping, half-inarticulate song. Only of late years have I noticed the shore larks in this section. Now they breed and pass the summer on these hills, and I am told that they are gradually becoming permanent residents in other parts of the State. They are nearly as large as the English skylark, with conspicuous black markings about the head and throat; shy birds squatting in the sere grass, and probably taken by most country people who see them to be sparrows.

Their flight and manner in song is much like that of the skylark. The bird mounts up and up on ecstatic wing, till it becomes a mere speck against the sky, where it drifts to and fro, and utters at intervals its crude song, a mere fraction or rudiment of the skylark's song, a few sharp, lisping, unmelodious notes, as if the bird had a bad cold, and could only now and then make any sound, — heard a long distance, but insignificant, a mere germ of the true lark's song; as it were the first rude attempt of nature in this direction. After due trial and waiting, it develops the lark's song itself. But if the law of evolution applies to bird-songs as well as to other things, the shore lark should in time become a fine songster. I know of no bird-song that seems so obviously struggling to free itself and reach a fuller expression. As the bird seems more and more inclined to abide permanently amid cultivated fields, and to forsake the wild and savage north, let us hope that its song is also undergoing a favorable change.

How conspicuous the crows in the brown fields, or against the lingering snow-banks, or in the clear sky! How still the air! One could carry a lighted candle over the hills. The light is very strong, and the effect of the wall of white mountains rising up all around from the checkered landscape, and holding up the blue dome of the sky, is strange indeed.

April 14. A delicious day, warm as May. This to me is the most bewitching part of the whole year. One's relish is so keen, and the morsels are so few and so tender. How the fields of winter rye stand out! They call up visions of England. A perfect day in April far excels a perfect day in June, because it provokes and stimulates while the latter sates and cloys. Such days have all the peace and geniality of summer without any of its satiety or enervating heat.

April 15. Not much cloud this morning, but much vapor in the air. A cool south wind with streaks of a pungent vegetable odor, probably from the willows. When I make too dead a set at it, I miss it; but when I let my nose have its own way, and take in the air slowly, I get it, an odor as of a myriad swelling buds. The long-drawn call of the high-hole comes up from the fields, then the tender rapid trill of the bush or russet sparrow, then the piercing note of the meadowlark, a flying shaft of sound.

April 21. The enchanting days continue without a break. One's senses are not large enough to take them all in. Maple buds just bursting, apple-trees full of infantile leaves. How the poplars and willows stand out! A moist, warm, brooding haze over all the earth. All day my little russet sparrow sings and trills divinely. The most prominent bird music in April is from the sparrows.

The yellowbirds (goldfinches) are just getting on their yellow coats. I saw some yesterday that had a smutty, unwashed look, because of the new yellow shining through the old drab-colored webs of the feathers. These birds do not shed their feathers in the spring, as careless observers are apt to think they do, but merely shed the outer webs of their feathers and quills, which peel off like a glove from the hand.

All the groves and woods lightly touched with new foliage. Looks like May; violets and dandelions in bloom. Sparrow's nest with two eggs. Maples hanging out their delicate fringe-like bloom. First barn swallows may be looked for any day after April 20.

This period may be called the vernal equipoise, and corresponds to the October calm called the Indian summer.

April 2, 1890. The second of the April days, clear as a bell. The eye of the heavens wide open at last. A sparrow day; how they sang! And the robins, too, before I was up in the morning. Now and then I could hear the rat-tat-tat of the downy at his drum. How many times I paused at my work to drink in the beauty of the day!

How I like to walk out after supper these days! I stroll over the lawn and stand on the brink of the hill. The sun is down, the robins pipe and call, and as the dusk comes on, they indulge in that loud chiding note or scream, whether in anger or in fun I never can tell. Up the road in the distance the multitudinous voice of the little peepers, — a thicket or screen of sound. An April twilight is unlike any other.

April 12. Lovely, bright day. We plow the ground under the hill for the new vineyard. In opening the furrow for the young vines I guide the team by walking in their front. How I soaked up the sunshine to-day! At night I glowed all over; my whole being had had an earth-bath; such a feeling of freshly plowed land in every cell of my brain. The furrow had struck in; the sunshine had photographed it upon my soul.

April 13. A warm, even hot April day. The air full of haze; the sunshine golden. In the afternoon J. and I walk out over the country north of town. Everybody is out, all the paths and byways are full of boys and young fellows. We sit on a wall a long time by a meadow and an orchard, and drink in the scene. April to perfection, such a sentiment of spring everywhere. The sky is partly overcast, the air moist, just enough so to bring out the odors, — a sweet perfume of bursting, growing things. One could almost eat the turf like a horse. All about the robins sang. In the trees the crow blackbird cackled and jingled. Athwart these sounds came every half minute the clear, strong note of the meadowlark. The larks were very numerous and were lovemaking. Then the high-hole called and the bush sparrow trilled. Arbutus days these, everybody wants to go to the woods for arbutus; it fairly calls one. The soil calls for the plow, too, the garden calls for the spade, the vineyard calls for the hoe. From all about the farm voices call, Come and do this, or do that. At night, how the "peepers" pile up the sound!

How I delight to see the plow at work such mornings! the earth is ripe for it, fairly lusts for it, and the freshly turned soil looks good enough to eat.

Plucked my first blood-root this morning, — a full-blown flower with a young one folded up in a leaf beneath it, only the bud emerging, like the head of a pappoose protruding from its mother's blanket, — a very pretty sight. The blood-root always comes up with the leaf shielding the flower-bud, as one shields the flame of the candle in the open air with his hand half closed about it.

These days the song of the toad — *tr-r-r-r-r-r-r-r-r-r-r-r-r-r-r-r-r-r-r-r* — is heard in the land. At nearly all hours I hear it, and it is as welcome to me as the song of any bird. It is a kind of gossamer of sound drifting in the air. Mother toad is in the pools and puddles now depositing that long chain or raveling of eggs, while her dapper little mate rides upon her back and fertilizes them as they are laid. As I look toward the fields where the first brown thrasher is singing, I see emerald patches of rye. The unctuous, confident strain of the bird seems to make the fields grow greener hour by hour.

May 4. The perfection of early May weather. How green the grass, how happy the birds, how placid the river, how busy the bees, how soft the air! — that kind of weather when there seems to be dew in the air all day, — the day a kind of prolonged morning, — so fresh, so wooing, so caressing! The baby leaves on the apple-trees have doubled in size since last night.

March 12, 1891. Had positive proof this morning that at least one song sparrow has come back to his haunts of a year ago. One year ago to-day my attention was attracted, while walking over to the post-office, by an unfamiliar bird-song. It caught my ear while I was a long way off. I followed it up and found that it proceeded from a song sparrow. Its chief feature was one long, clear high note, very strong, sweet, and plaintive. It sprang out of the trills and quavers of the first part of the bird-song, like a long arc or parabola of sound. To my mental vision it rose far up against the blue, and turned sharply downward again and finished in more trills and quavers. I had never before heard anything like it. It was the usual long, silvery note in the sparrow's song greatly increased; indeed, the whole breath and force of the bird were put in this note, so that you caught little else than this silver loop of sound. The bird remained in one locality — the bushy corner of a field — the whole season. He indulged in the ordinary sparrow song, also. I had repeatedly had my eye upon him when he changed from one to the other.

And now here he is again, just a year after, in the same place, singing the same remarkable song, capturing my ear with the same exquisite lasso of sound. What would I not give to know just where he passed the winter, and what adventures by flood and field befell him!

(I will add that the bird continued in song the

whole season, apparently confining his wanderings to a few acres of ground. But the following spring he did not return, and I have never heard him since, and if any of his progeny inherited this peculiar song, I have not heard them.)

Flicker

THE SPRING BIRD PROCESSION

ONE of the new pleasures of country life when one has made the acquaintance of the birds is to witness the northward bird procession as it passes or tarries with us in the spring — a procession which lasts from April till June and has some new feature daily.

The migrating wild creatures, whether birds or beasts, always arrest the attention. They seem to link up animal life with the great currents of the globe. It is moving day on a continental scale. It is the call of the primal instinct to increase and multiply, suddenly setting in motion whole tribes and races. The first phœbe-bird, the first song sparrow, the first robin or bluebird in March or early April, is like the first ripple of the rising tide on the shore.

In my boyhood the vast armies of the passenger pigeons were one of the most notable spring tokens. Often late in March, or early in April, the naked beechwoods would suddenly become blue with them, and vocal with their soft, childlike calls; or all day the sky would be streaked with the long lines or dense masses of the moving armies. The last great flight of them that I ever beheld was on the 10th of April, 1875, when, for the greater part of the day, one could not at any moment look skyward above the Hudson River Valley without seeing several flocks, great and small, of the migrating birds. But that spectacle was never repeated as it had been for generations before. The pigeons never came back. Death and destruction, in the shape of the greed and cupidity of man, were on their trail. The hosts were pursued from State to State by professional pot-hunters and netters, and the numbers so reduced, and their flocking instinct so disorganized, that their vast migrating bands disappeared, and they were seen only in loosely scattered and diminishing flocks in different parts of the West during the remainder of the century. A friend of mine shot a few in Indiana in the early eighties, and scattered bands of them have occasionally been reported, here and there, up to within a few years. The last time that my eyes beheld a passenger pigeon was in the fall of 1876 when I was out for grouse. I saw a solitary cock sitting in a tree. I killed it, little dreaming that, so far as I was concerned, I was killing the last pigeon.

What man now in his old age who witnessed in youth that spring or fall festival and migration of the passenger pigeons would not hail it as one of the gladdest hours of his life if he could be permitted to witness it once more? It was such a spectacle of bounty, of joyous, copious animal life, of fertility in the air and in the wilderness, as to make the heart glad. I have seen the fields and woods fairly inundated for a day or two with these fluttering, piping, blue-and-white hosts. The very air at times seemed suddenly to turn to pigeons.

One May evening recently, near sundown, as I sat in my summer-house here in the Hudson Valley, I saw a long, curved line of migrating fowl high in the air, moving with great speed northward, and for a moment I felt the old thrill that I used to experience on beholding the pigeons. Fifty years ago I should have felt sure that they were pigeons; but they were only ducks. A more intense scrutiny failed to reveal the sharp, arrow-like effect of a swiftly moving flock of pigeons. The rounder, bottle-shaped bodies of the ducks also became apparent. But migrating ducks are a pleasing spectacle, and when, a little later, a line of geese came into my field of vision, and re-formed and trimmed their ranks there against the rosy sky above me, and drove northward with their masterly flight, there was no suggestion of the barnyard or farm pond up there.

"Whither, midst falling dew,
While glow the heavens with the last steps of day,

THE BIRDS OF JOHN BURROUGHS

Far, through their rosy depths, dost thou pursue
Thy solitary way?"

Bryant, by the way, handled natural subjects in a large, free, simple way, which our younger poets never attained.

When one is fortunate enough to see a line of swans etched upon the sky near sunset, a mile or more high, as has been my luck but twice in my life, one has seen something he will not soon forget.

The northward movement of the smaller bodies — the warblers and finches and thrushes — gives one pleasure of a different kind, the pleasure of rare and distinguished visitors who tarry for a few hours or a few days, enlivening the groves and orchards and garden borders, and then pass on. Delicacy of color, grace of form, animation of movement, and often snatches of song, and elusive notes and calls, advise the bird-lover that the fairy procession is arriving. Tiny guests from Central and South America drop out of the sky like flowers borne by the night winds, and give unwonted interest to our tree-tops and roadside hedges. The ruby-crowned kinglet heralds the approach of the procession, morning after morning, by sounding his elfin bugle in the evergreens.

The migrating thrushes in passing are much more chary of their songs, although the hermit, the veery, and the olive-backed may occasionally be heard. I have even heard the northern water-thrush sing briefly in my currant-patch. The bobolink begins to burst out in sudden snatches of song, high in air, as he nears his northern haunts. I have often in May heard the black-poll warbler deliver his fine strain, like that of some ticking insect, but have never heard the bay-breasted nor the speckled Canada during migration. None of these birds sing or nest in the tropical countries where they pass more than half the year. They are like exiles there; the joy and color fade out of their lives in the land of color and luxuriance. The brilliant tints come to their plumage, and the songs to their hearts, only when the breeding impulse sends them to their brief northern homes. Tennyson makes his swallow say, —

"I do but wanton in the South,
    While in the North long since my nest is made."

It is highly probable, if not certain, that the matches made in the North endure but for a season, and that new mates are chosen each spring. The males of most species come a few days in advance of the females, being, I suppose, supercharged with the breeding impulse.

That birds have a sense of home and return in most cases to their old haunts, is quite certain. But whether both sexes do this, or only the males, I have no proof. But I have proof which I consider positive that the male song sparrow returns, and there is pretty good evidence that the same thing is true of several, probably of most, other species. A friend of mine has a summer home in one of the more secluded valleys of the Catskills, and every June for three years a pair of catbirds have nested near the house; and every day, many times, one or both birds come to the dining-room window, for sweet butter. Very soon after their arrival they appear at the window, shy at first, but soon becoming so tame that they approach within a few feet of the mistress of the house. They light on the chairbacks and sometimes even hop on the table, taking the butter from the fork held by the mistress. Their behavior now is very convincing that one or both have been at the window for butter in previous years.

Let me quote a page or two from my notebook, under date of May 25: —

Walked down through the fields and woods to the river, and then along the wooded banks toward home.

Redstarts here and there in the woods, going through their pretty gymnastics. None of our insect-feeders known to me so engage the eye. The flashes of color, and the acrobatic feats — how they set each other off! It is all so much like a premeditated display, or a circus, or an operatic performance, that one is surprised to find a solitary bird in the woods so intent upon it. Every movement is accompanied by its own feathered display. The tail, with its bands of black and orange, is as active in opening and shutting as a lady's fan at the opera signaling to her lover; the wings unfold, or droop, and second the sensitive tail, and the whole behavior of the bird makes him about the prettiest actor in the little fly-catching drama of the season. This behavior would suggest that the bird feeds upon a particular kind of insect; at all times and places it is engaged in the same striking acrobatic feats; just as the black and white creeping warbler is always busy in the hunt for some minute insect on the trunks of trees.

I recall several of our insect-feeders each of which seems to have its own insect province. The Kentucky warbler, where I have known it on the Potomac, fed for the most part on insects which it gathered from the under side of the leaves of certain plants near the ground. Hence it is classed among the ground warblers, like the Maryland yellow-throat. The red-eyed vireo feeds largely on the insects which hide on the under side of leaves in the tree-tops.

When the oriole first comes in May, he is very busy searching into the heart of the apple-tree bloom for some small insect. I have seen Wilson's black-capped warbler doing the same thing. I have seen a score or more of myrtle warblers very active amid the bushes and trees along a stream, snapping up some slow-moving gauzy insect drifting about there. They often festoon the stream with their curving and looping lines of blue and black and yellow.

The feeding-ground of one bird is often an empty

larder to another kind. I saw a pretty illustration of this fact yesterday. On the wide, smooth space, graded with sharp gravel in front of my neighbor's boathouse, there were three Blackburnian warblers, one male and two females, very much absorbed in hurrying about over the gray surface, picking up some tiny insects which were invisible to my eye. How intent and eager they were! A nuthatch came down the trunk of the elm and eyed them closely; then took to the ground and followed them about for a moment. But evidently he could not make out what the table was spread with, as, after a few seconds, he flew back to the tree and went on with his own quest of food. But the nuthatches will follow the downy woodpeckers through the trees, and the chickadees follow the nuthatches, and the brown creepers follow the chickadees, and each kind appears to find the food it is looking for. Every man to his taste, and every bird to the food that its beak indicates.

I have no idea as to the kind of food that invariably draws the male scarlet tanager to the ground in the ploughed fields at this season; but there they are in pairs or triplets, slowly looking over the brown soil and visible from afar. Yesterday I came upon two on the ground at a wettish place in the woods, demurely looking about them. How they fairly warmed the eye amid their dull and neutral surroundings!

Season after season, all over the country, the spectacle of scarlet tanagers inspecting the ground in ploughed fields recurs.

This season an unusual number of male rose-breasted grosbeaks have frequented the ground in my vineyards at the same time. Their black-and-white plumage, with an occasional glimpse of their rose-colored breasts, makes them very noticeable, but not so conspicuous as the tanagers. But their rich, mellow warblings from the tree-tops more than make up to the ear what the eye misses. Strange to say, in my boyhood I never saw or recognized this bird, and few country or farm people, I think, ever discriminate it. Its song is like that of the robin much softened and rounded and more finely modulated, contrasting in this respect with the harder and more midsummery strain of the tanager. The heavy beak of the bird gives him a somewhat Hebraic look.

II

That birds of a feather flock together, even in migration, is evident enough every spring. When in the morning you see one of a kind, you may confidently look for many more. When, in early May, I see one myrtle warbler, I presently see dozens of them in the trees and bushes all about me; or, if I see one yellow redpoll on the ground, with its sharp chirp and nervous behavior, I look for more. Yes-

terday, out of the kitchen window, I saw three
speckled Canada warblers on the ground in the
garden. How choice and rare they looked on the
dull surface! In my neighbor's garden or dooryard
I should probably have seen more of them, and
in his trees and shrubbery as many magnolia and
bay-breasted and black-throated blue warblers as
in my own; and about his neighbor's place, and
his, and his, throughout the township, and on west
throughout the county, and throughout the State,
and the adjoining State, on west to the Mississippi and beyond, I should have found in every
bushy tangle and roadside and orchard and grove
and wood and brookside, the same advancing line
of migrating birds — warblers, flycatchers, finches,
thrushes, sparrows, and so on — that I found here.
I should have found high-holes calling and drumming, robins and phœbes nesting, swallows skim-
ming, orioles piping, oven-birds demurely tripping
over the leaves in the woods, tanagers and grosbeaks in the ploughed fields, purple finches in the
cherry-trees, and white-throats and white-crowned
sparrows in the hedges.

One sees the passing bird procession in his own
grounds and neighborhood without pausing to think
that in every man's grounds and in every neighborhood throughout the State, and throughout a
long, broad belt of States, about several millions
of homes, and over several millions of farms, the

same flood-tide of bird-life is creeping and eddying or sweeping over the land. When the mating or nesting high-holes are awakening you in the early morning by their insistent calling and drumming on your metal roof or gutters or ridge-boards, they are doing the same to your neighbors near by, and to your fellow countrymen fifty, a hundred, a thousand miles away. Think of the myriads of dooryards where the "chippies" are just arriving; of the blooming orchards where the passing many-colored warblers are eagerly inspecting the buds and leaves; of the woods and woody streams where the oven-birds and water-thrushes are searching out their old haunts; of the secluded bushy fields and tangles where the chewinks, the brown thrashers, the chats, the catbirds, are once more preparing to begin life anew — think of all this and more, and you may get some idea of the extent and importance of our bird-life.

I fancy that on almost any day in mid-May the flickers are drilling their holes into a million or more decayed trees between the Hudson and the Mississippi; that any day a month earlier the phœbes are starting their nests under a million or more woodsheds or bridges or overhanging rocks; that several millions of robins are carrying mud and straws to sheltered projections about buildings, or to the big forked branches in the orchards.

When in my walk one day in April, through an

old cedar lane, I found a mourning dove's nest on the top of an old stone wall, — the only one I ever found in such a position, — I wondered how many mourning doves throughout the breadth and length of the land had built or were then building their nests on stone walls or on rocks.

Considering the enormous number of birds of all species that flood the continent at this season, as if some dike or barrier south of us had suddenly given way, one wonders where they could all have been pent up during the winter. Mexico and Central and South America have their own bird populations the seasons through; and with the addition of the hosts from this country, it seems as if those lands must have literally swarmed with birds, and that the food question (as with us) must have been pressing. Of course, a great many of our birds — such as sparrows, robins, blackbirds, meadowlarks, jays, and chewinks — spend the winter in the Southern States, but many more — warblers, swallows, swifts, hummers, orioles, tanagers, cuckoos, flycatchers, vireos, and others — seek out the equatorial region.

III

The ever-memorable war spring of 1917 was very backward, — about two weeks later than the average, — very cold, and very wet. Few fruit-trees bloomed before the 20th of May; then they all bloomed together: cherry, pear, peach, apple, all held back till they could stand it no longer. Pink peach-orchards and white apple-orchards at the same time and place made an unusual spectacle.

The cold, wet weather, of course, held up the bird procession also. The warblers and other migrants lingered and accumulated. The question of food became a very serious one with all the insect-eaters. The insects did not hatch, or, if they did, they kept very close to cover. The warblers, driven from the trees, took to the ground. It was an unusual spectacle to see these delicate and many-colored spirits of the air and of the tree-tops hopping about amid the clods and the rubbish, searching for something they could eat. They were like jewels in the gutter, or flowers on the sidewalk.

For several days in succession I saw several speckled Canada warblers hopping about my newly planted garden, evidently with poor results; then it was two or more Blackburnian warblers looking over the same ground, their new black-and-white and vivid orange plumage fairly illuminating the dull surface. The redstarts flashed along the ground and about the low bushes and around the outbuildings, delighting the eye in the same way. Bay-breasted warblers tarried and tarried, now on the ground, now in the lower branches of the trees or in bushes. I sat by a rapid rocky stream one afternoon and watched for half an hour a score or more of myrtle warblers snapping up the gauzy-winged insects that hovered above the water in the fitful sunshine. What loops and lines of color they made, now perched on the stones, now on the twigs of the overhanging trees, now hovering, now swooping! What an animated scene they presented! They had struck a rare find and were making the most of it.

On other occasions I saw the magnolia and Cape May and chestnut-sided warblers under the same stress of food-shortage searching in unwonted places. One bedraggled and half-starved female magnolia warbler lingered eight or ten days in a row of Japanese barberry-bushes under my window, where she seemed to find some minute and, to me, invisible insect on the leaves and in the blossoms that seemed worth her while.

This row of barberry-bushes was the haunt for a week or more of two or three male ruby-throated hummingbirds. Not one female did we see, but two males were often there at the same time, and sometimes three. They came at all hours and probed the clusters of small greenish-yellow blossoms, and perched on the twigs of intermingled lilacs, often remaining at rest five or six minutes at a time. They chased away the big queen bumble-bees which also reaped a harvest there, and occasionally darted spitefully at each other. The first day I saw them, they appeared to be greatly fatigued, as if they had just made the long journey from Central

America. Never before had I seen this bird-jewel of omnipotent wing take so kindly and so habituatedly to the perch.

The unseasonable season, no doubt, caused the death of vast numbers of warblers. We picked up two about the paths on my place, and the neighbors found dead birds about their grounds. Often live birds were so reduced in vitality that they allowed the passer-by to pick them up. Where one dead bird was seen, no doubt hundreds escaped notice in the fields and groves. A bird lives so intensely — rapid breathing and high temperature — that its need for food is always pressing. These adventurous little aviators had come all the way from South and Central America; the fuel-supply of their tiny engines was very low, and they suffered accordingly.

A friend writing me from Maine at this time had the same story of famishing warblers to tell. Certain of our more robust birds suffered. A male oriole came under my window one morning and pecked a long time at a dry crust of bread—a food, I dare say, it had never tasted before. The robins alone were in high feather. The crop of angleworms was one hundred per cent, and one could see the robins "snaking" them out of the ground at all hours.

Emerson is happy in his epithet "the punctual birds." They are nearly always here on time — always, considering the stage of the season; but the inflexible calendar often finds them late or early.

There is one bird, however, that keeps pretty close
to the calendar. I refer to the white-crowned sparrow, the most distinguished-looking of all our sparrows. Year after year, be the season early or late,
I am on the lookout for him between the 12th and
the 16th of May. This year, on the 13th, I looked
out of my kitchen window and saw two males hopping along side by side in the garden. Unhurriedly
they moved about, unconscious of their shapely
forms and fine bearing. Their black-and-white
crowns, their finely penciled backs, their pure ashen-
gray breasts, and their pretty carriage, give them a
decided look of distinction. Such a contrast to our
nervous and fidgety song sparrow, bless her little
heart! And how different from the more chunky
and plebeian-looking white-throats — bless their
hearts also for their longer tarrying and their sweet,
quavering ribbon of song! The fox sparrow, the
most brilliant singer of all our sparrows, is an uncertain visitor in the Hudson River Valley, and seasons pass without one glimpse of him.

The spring of 1917 was remarkable for the number of migrating blue jays. For many days in May
I beheld the unusual spectacle of processions of jays
streaming northward. Considering the numbers I
saw during the short time in the morning that I was
in the open, if the numbers I did not see were in like
proportion, many thousands of them must have
passed my outlook northward. The jay is evidently

more or less a migrant. I saw not one here during the winter, which is unusual. As one goes south in winter the number of jays greatly increases, till in Georgia they are nearly as abundant as robins are here in summer.

In late April a friend wrote me from a town in northern New York that the high-holes disturbed his sleep in the early morning by incessant drumming on the metal roofs and gutters and ridge-boards. They were making the same racket around us at the same hour. Early in the month a pair of them seem to have been attracted to a cavity in the mid-top of a maple-tree near the house, and the male began to warm up under the fever of the nesting-impulse, till he made himself quite a nuisance to sleepers who did not like to be drummed out before five o'clock in the morning. How loudly he did publish and proclaim his joy in the old command which spring always reaffirms in all creatures! With call and drum, repeated to the weariness of his less responsive neighbors, he made known the glad tidings from his perch on the verge of the tin roof; he would send forth the loud, rapid call, which, as Thoreau aptly says, has the effect as of some one suddenly opening a window and calling in breathless haste, "Quick, quick, quick, quick!" Then he would bow his head and pour a volley of raps upon the wood or metal, which became a continuous stream of ringing blows. One would have thought that he had a steel punch for a bill, and that it never got dull.

But the high-hole's bill is a wonderful instrument and serves him in many ways. In the spring bird-orchestra he plays an important part, more so than that of any other of the woodpeckers. He is never a disturber of the country quiet except on such occasions as above referred to. His insistent call coming up from the April and May meadows or pastures or groves is pleasing to the nature-lover to a high degree. It does seem to quicken the season's coming, though my pair were slow in getting down to business, doubtless on account of the backward spring and the consequent scarcity of ants, which are their favorite food.

When on the 1st of June I looked into the cavity in one of my maples, and saw only one egg, I thought it a meagre result for all that month and a half of beating of drum and clashing of cymbals; but on the 20th of June the results were more ample, and four open mouths greeted me as I again looked into the little dark chamber in the maple. The drumming and trumpeting had ceased, and the festive and holiday air of the birds had given place to an air of silent solicitude. As the cavity is a natural one, the result of a decayed limb, it does not have the carpeting of soft pulverized "dozy" wood that it would have had it been excavated by the birds. Hence, for days before the full complement of eggs was laid, and after the young had hatched, I used to see and hear, as I passed by, one of the parent birds pecking on the sides of the cavity, evidently to loosen material to supply this deficiency.

The high-hole is our most abundant species of woodpecker, and as he gets most of his living from the ground instead of from the trees, he is a migrant in the Northern States. Our other members of the family are mostly black, white, and red, but the high-hole is colored very much like the meadowlark, in mottled browns and whites and yellows, with a dash of red on the nape of his neck. To his enemies in the air he is not a conspicuous object on the ground, as the other species would be.

IV

The waves of bird migrants roll on through the States into Canada and beyond, breaking like waves on the shore, and spreading their contents over large areas. The warbler wave spends itself largely in the forests and mountains of the northern tier of States and of Canada; its utmost range, in the shape of the pileolated warbler (the Western form of Wilson's black-cap) and a few others, reaching beyond the Arctic Circle, while its content of ground warblers, in the shape of the Maryland yellow-throat and the Kentucky and the hooded warblers, begins to drop out south of the Potomac and in Ohio.

The robins cover a very wide area, as do the song sparrows, the kingbirds, the vireos, the flickers, the orioles, the catbirds, and others. The area covered by the bobolinks is fast becoming less and less, or at least it is moving farther and farther north. Bobolinks in New York State meadows are becoming rare birds, but in Canadian meadows they appear to be on the increase. The mowing-machine and the earlier gathering of the hay-crop by ten or fourteen days than fifty years ago probably account for it.

As the birds begin to arrive from the South in the spring, the birds that have come down from the North to spend the winter with us — the crossbills, the pine grosbeaks, the pine linnets, the red-breasted nuthatches, the juncos, and the snow buntings — begin to withdraw. The ebb of one species follows the flow of another. One winter, in December, a solitary red-breasted nuthatch took up his abode with me, attracted by the suet and nuts I had placed on a maple-tree-trunk in front of my study window for the downy woodpecker, the chickadees, and the native nuthatches. Red-breast evidently said to himself, "Needless to look farther." He took lodgings in a wren-box on a post near by, and at night and during windy, stormy days was securely housed there. He tarried till April, and his constancy, his pretty form, and his engaging ways greatly endeared him to us. The pair of white-breasted nuthatches that fed at the same table looked coarse and common beside this little delicate waif from the far North. He could not stand to see lying about a superabundance of cracked hickory-nuts, any more than his larger relatives could, and would work industriously, carrying them away and hiding them in the woodpile and summer-house near by. The other nuthatches bossed him, as they in turn were bossed by Downy, and as he in turn bossed the brown creeper and the chickadees. In early April my little red-breast disappeared, and I fancied him turning his face northward, urged by a stronger impulse than that for food and shelter merely. He was my tiny guest from unknown lands, my baby bird, and he left a vacancy that none of the others could fill.

The nuthatches are much more pleasing than the woodpeckers. Soft-voiced, soft-colored, gentle-mannered, they glide over the rough branches and the tree-trunks with their boat-shaped bodies, going up and down and around, with apparently an extra joint in their necks that enables them, head-downward, to look straight out from the tree-trunk; their motions seem far less mechanical and angular than those of the woodpeckers and the creepers. Downy can back down a tree by short hitches, but he never ventures to do it headfirst, nor does the creeper; but the universal joint in the nuthatch's body and its rounded keel enable it to move head on indifferently in all directions. Its soft nasal call in the spring woods is one of the most welcome of sounds. It is like the voice of children, plaintive but contented, a soft interrogation in the ear of the sylvan gods. What a contrast to the sharp, steely note of the woodpeckers — the hairy's like the metallic sounds of the tinsmith and Downy's a minor key of the same!

But the woodpeckers have their drums which make the dry limbs vocal, and hint the universal spring awakening in a very agreeable manner. The two sounds together, the childish "Yank, yank," of the nuthatch, and the resonant "Rat-tat-tat" of Downy, are coincident with the stirring sap in the maple trees. The robin, the bluebird, the song sparrow, and the phoebe have already loosened the fetters of winter in the open. It is interesting to note how differently the woodpeckers and the nuthatches use their beaks in procuring their food. Downy's head is a trip-hammer, and he drives his beak into the wood by short, sharp blows, making the chips fly, while the nuthatch strikes more softly, using his whole body in the movement. He delivers a kind of feathered blow on the fragment of nut which he has placed in the vise of the tree's bark. My little redbreast, previously referred to, came down on a nut in the same way, with a pretty extra touch of the flash of his wings at each stroke, as the woodchopper says "Hah!" when sending his axe home.

If this does not add force to his blows, it certainly emphasizes them in a very pretty manner.

Each species of wild creature has its own individual ways and idiosyncrasies which one likes to note. As I write these lines a male kingbird flies by the apple-tree in which his mate is building a nest, with that peculiar mincing and affected flight which none other of the flycatchers, so far as I know, ever assumes. The olive-sided flycatcher has his own little trick, too, which the others do not have: I have seen his whole appearance suddenly change while sitting on a limb, by the exhibition of a band of white feathers like a broad chalk-mark outlining his body. Apparently the white feathers under the wings could be projected at will, completely transforming the appearance of the bird. He would change in a twinkling from a dark, motionless object to one surrounded by a broad band of white.

It occasionally happens that a familiar bird develops an unfamiliar trait. The purple finch is one of our sweetest songsters and best-behaved birds, but one that escapes the attention of most country people. But the past season he made himself conspicuous with us by covering the ground beneath the cherry-trees with cherry-blossoms. Being hard put to it for food, a flock of the birds must have discovered that every cherry-blossom held a tidbit in the shape of its ovary. At once the birds began to cut out these ovaries, soon making the ground white beneath the trees. I grew alarmed for the safety of my crop of Windsors, and tried to "shoo" the birds away. They looked down upon me as if they considered it a good joke. Even when we shot one, to make sure of the identity of the bird, the flock only flew to the next tree and went on with the snipping. Beneath two cherry-trees that stood beside the highway the blossoms drifted into the wagon tracks like snowflakes. I concluded that the birds had taken very heavy toll of my cherries, but it turned out that they had only done a little of the much-needed thinning. Out of a cluster of six or eight blossoms they seldom took more than two or three, as if they knew precisely what they were about, and were intent on rendering me a service. When the robins and the cedar-birds come for the cherries they are not so considerate, but make a clean sweep. The finches could teach them manners — and morals.

WILD LIFE ABOUT MY CABIN

FRIENDS have often asked me why I turned my back upon the Hudson and retreated into the wilderness. Well, I do not call it a retreat; I call it a withdrawal, a retirement, the taking up of a new position to renew the attack, it may be, more vigorously than ever. It is not always easy to give reasons. There are reasons within reasons, and often no reasons at all that we are aware of.

To a countryman like myself, not born to a great river or an extensive water-view, these things, I think, grow wearisome after a time. He becomes surfeited with a beauty that is alien to him. He longs for something more homely, private, and secluded. Scenery may be too fine or too grand and imposing for one's daily and hourly view. It tires after a while. It demands a mood that comes to you only at intervals. Hence it is never wise to build your house on the most ambitious spot in the landscape. Rather seek out a more humble and secluded nook or corner, which you can fill and warm with your domestic and home instincts and affections. In some things the half is often more satisfying than the whole. A

117

Whip-poor-will

glimpse of the Hudson River between hills or through openings in the trees wears better with me than a long expanse of it constantly spread out before me. One day I had an errand to a farmhouse nestled in a little valley or basin at the foot of a mountain. The earth put out protecting arms all about it, — a low hill with an orchard on one side, a sloping pasture on another, and the mountain, with the skirts of its mantling forests, close at hand in the rear. How my heart warmed toward it! I had been so long perched high upon the banks of a great river, in sight of all the world, exposed to every wind that blows, with a horizon-line that sweeps over half a county, that, quite unconsciously to myself, I was pining for a nook to sit down in. I was hungry for the private and the circumscribed; I knew it when I saw this sheltered farmstead. I had long been restless and dissatisfied, — a vague kind of homesickness; now I knew the remedy. Hence when, not long afterward, I was offered a tract of wild land, barely a mile from home, that contained a secluded nook and a few acres of level, fertile land shut off from the vain and noisy world of railroads, steamboats, and yachts by a wooded, precipitous mountain, I quickly closed the bargain, and built me a rustic house there, which I call "Slabsides," because its outer walls are covered with slabs. I might have given it a prettier name, but not one more fit, or more in keeping with the mood that brought me thither.

A slab is the first cut from the log, and the bark goes with it. It is like the first cut from the loaf, which we call the crust, and which the children reject, but which we older ones often prefer. I wanted to take a fresh cut of life, — something that had the bark on, or, if you please, that was like a well-browned and hardened crust. After three years I am satisfied with the experiment. Life has a different flavor here. It is reduced to simpler terms; its complex equations all disappear. The exact value of x may still elude me, but I can press it hard; I have shorn it of many of its disguises and entanglements.

When I went into the woods the robins went with me, or rather they followed close. As soon as a space of ground was cleared and the garden planted, they were on hand to pick up the worms and insects, and to superintend the planting of the cherry-trees: three pairs the first summer, and more than double that number the second. In the third, their early morning chorus was almost as marked a feature as it is about the old farm homesteads. The robin is no hermit: he likes company; he likes the busy scenes of the farm and the village; he likes to carol to listening ears, and to build his nest as near your dwelling as he can. Only at rare intervals do I find a real sylvan robin, one that nests in the woods, usually by still waters, remote from human habitation. In such places his morning and evening carol is a welcome surprise to the fisherman or camper-out. It is like a dooryard flower found blooming in the wilderness. With the robins came the song sparrows and social sparrows, or chippies, also. The latter nested in the bushes near my cabin, and the song sparrows in the bank above the ditch that drains my land. I notice that Chippy finds just as many horsehairs to weave into her nest here in my horseless domain as she does when she builds in the open country. Her partiality for the long hairs from the manes and tails of horses and cattle is so great that she is often known as the hair-bird. What would she do in a country where there were neither cows nor horses? Yet these hairs are not good nesting-material. They are slippery, refractory things, and occasionally cause a tragedy in the nest by getting looped around the legs or the neck of the young or of the parent bird. They probably give a smooth finish to the interior, dear to the heart of Chippy.

The first year of my cabin life a pair of robins attempted to build a nest upon the round timber that forms the plate under my porch roof. But it was a poor place to build in. It took nearly a week's time and caused the birds a great waste of labor to find this out. The coarse material they brought for the foundation would not bed well upon the rounded surface of the timber, and every vagrant breeze that came along swept it off. My porch was kept littered with twigs and weed-stalks for days, till finally the birds abandoned the undertaking. The next season a wiser or more experienced pair made the attempt again, and succeeded. They placed the nest against the rafter where it joins the plate; they used mud from the start to level up with and to hold the first twigs and straws, and had soon completed a firm, shapely structure. When the young were about ready to fly, it was interesting to note that there was apparently an older and a younger, as in most families. One bird was more advanced than any of the others. Had the parent birds intentionally stimulated it with extra quantities of food, so as to be able to launch their offspring into the world one at a time? At any rate, one of the birds was ready to leave the nest a day and a half before any of the others. I happened to be looking at it when the first impulse to get outside the nest seemed to seize it. Its parents were encouraging it with calls and assurances from some rocks a few yards away. It answered their calls in vigorous, strident tones. Then it climbed over the edge of the nest upon the plate, took a few steps forward, then a few more, till it was a yard from the nest and near the end of the timber, and could look off into free space. Its parents apparently shouted, "Come on!" But its courage was not quite equal to the leap; it looked around, and seeing how far it was from home, scampered back to the nest, and climbed into it like a frightened child. It had made its first journey into the world, but the home tie had brought it quickly back.

A few hours afterward it journeyed to the end of the plate again, and then turned and rushed back. The third time its heart was braver, its wings stronger, and leaping into the air with a shout, it flew easily to some rocks a dozen or more yards away. Each of the young in succession, at intervals of nearly a day, left the nest in this manner. There would be the first journey of a few feet along the plate, the first sudden panic at being so far from home, the rush back, a second and perhaps a third attempt, and then the irrevocable leap into the air, and a clamorous flight to a near-by bush or rock. Young birds never go back when they have once taken flight. The first free flap of the wing severs forever the ties that bind them to home.

The chickadees we have always with us. They are like the evergreens among the trees and plants. Winter has no terrors for them. They are properly wood-birds, but the groves and orchards know them also. Did they come near my cabin for better protection, or did they chance to find a little cavity in a tree there that suited them? Branch-builders and ground-builders are easily accommodated, but the chickadee must find a cavity, and a small one at that. The woodpeckers make a cavity when a suitable trunk or branch is found, but the chickadee, with its small, sharp beak, rarely does so; it usually smooths and deepens one already formed. This a pair did a few yards from my cabin. The opening was into the heart of a little sassafras, about four feet from the ground. Day after day the birds took turns in deepening and enlarging the cavity: a soft, gentle hammering for a few moments in the heart of the little tree, and then the appearance of the worker at the opening, with the chips in his, or her, beak. They changed off every little while, one working while the other gathered food. Absolute equality of the sexes, both in plumage and in duties, seems to prevail among these birds, as among a few other species. During the preparations for housekeeping the birds were hourly seen and heard, but as soon as the first egg was laid, all this was changed. They suddenly became very shy and quiet. Had it not been for the new egg that was added each day, one would have concluded that they had abandoned the place. There was a precious secret now that must be well kept. After incubation began, it was only by watching that I could get a glimpse of one of the birds as it came quickly to feed or to relieve the other.

One day a lot of Vassar girls came to visit me, and I led them out to the little sassafras to see the chickadees' nest. The sitting bird kept her place as head after head, with its nodding plumes and millinery, appeared above the opening to her chamber, and a pair of inquisitive eyes peered down upon her. But I saw that she was getting ready to play her little trick to frighten them away. Presently I heard a faint

explosion at the bottom of the cavity, when the peep-
ing girl jerked her head quickly back, with the ex-
clamation, "Why, it spit at me!" The trick of the
bird on such occasions is apparently to draw in its
breath till its form perceptibly swells, and then give
forth a quick, explosive sound like an escaping jet of
steam. One involuntarily closes his eyes and jerks
back his head. The girls, to their great amusement,
provoked the bird into this pretty outburst of her
impatience two or three times. But as the ruse failed
of its effect, the bird did not keep it up, but let the
laughing faces gaze till they were satisfied.

There is only one other bird known to me that
resorts to the same trick to scare away intruders,
and that is the great crested flycatcher. As your
head appears before the entrance to the cavity in
which the mother bird is sitting, a sudden burst of
escaping steam seems directed at your face, and
your backward movement leaves the way open for
the bird to escape, which she quickly does.

The chickadee is a prolific bird, laying from six
to eight eggs, and it seems to have few natural
enemies. I think it is seldom molested by squirrels
or black snakes or weasels or crows or owls. The
entrance to the nest is usually so small that none of
these creatures can come at them. Yet the number
of chickadees in any given territory seems small.
What keeps them in check? Probably the rigors of
winter and a limited food-supply. The ant-eaters,

fruit-eaters, and seed-eaters mostly migrate. Our all-the-year-round birds, like the chickadees, woodpeckers, jays, and nuthatches, live mostly on nuts and the eggs and larvæ of tree-insects, and hence their larder is a restricted one; hence, also, these birds rear only one brood in a season. A hairy woodpecker passed the winter in the woods near me by subsisting on a certain small white grub which he found in the bark of some dead hemlock-trees. He "worked" these trees, — four of them, — as the slang is, "for all they were worth." The grub was under the outer shell of bark, and the bird literally skinned the trees in getting at his favorite morsel. He worked from the top downward, hammering or prying off this shell, and leaving the trunk of the tree with a red, denuded look. Bushels of the fragments of the bark covered the ground at the foot of the tree in spring, and the trunk looked as if it had been flayed, — as it had.

The big chimney of my cabin of course attracted the chimney swifts, and as it was not used in summer, two pairs built their nests in it, and we had the muffled thunder of their wings at all hours of the day and night. One night, when one of the broods was nearly fledged, the nest that held them fell down into the fireplace. Such a din of screeching and chattering as they instantly set up! Neither my dog nor I could sleep. They yelled in chorus, stopping at the end of every half-minute as if upon signal. Now they were all screeching at the top of their voices, then a sudden, dead silence ensued. Then the din began again, to terminate at the instant as before. If they had been long practicing together, they could not have succeeded better. I never before heard the cry of birds so accurately timed. After a while I got up and put them back up the chimney, and stopped up the throat of the flue with newspapers. The next day one of the parent birds, in bringing food to them, came down the chimney with such force that it passed through the papers and brought up in the fireplace. On capturing it I saw that its throat was distended with food as a chipmunk's cheek with corn, or a boy's pocket with chestnuts. I opened its mandibles, when it ejected a wad of insects as large as a bean. Most of them were much macerated, but there were two house-flies yet alive and but little the worse for their close confinement. They stretched themselves, and walked about upon my hand, enjoying a breath of fresh air once more. It was nearly two hours before the swift again ventured into the chimney with food.

These birds do not perch, nor alight upon buildings or the ground. They are apparently upon the wing all day. They outride the storms. I have in my mind a cheering picture of three of them I saw facing a heavy thunder-shower one afternoon. The wind was blowing a gale, the clouds were rolling in black, portentous billows out of the west, the peals of thunder were shaking the heavens, and the big drops were just beginning to come down, when, on looking up, I saw three swifts high in air, working their way slowly, straight into the teeth of the storm. They were not hurried or disturbed; they held themselves firmly and steadily; indeed, they were fairly at anchor in the air till the rage of the elements should have subsided. I do not know that any other of our land birds outride the storms in this way.

The phœbe-birds also soon found me out in my retreat, and a pair of them deliberated a long while about building on a little shelf in one of my gables. But, much to my regret, they finally decided in favor of a niche in the face of a ledge of rocks not far from my spring. The place was well screened by bushes and well guarded against the approach of snakes or four-footed prowlers, and the birds prospered well and reared two broods. They have now occupied the same nest three years in succession. This is unusual: Phœbe prefers a new nest each season, but in this case there is no room for another, and, the site being a choice one, she slightly repairs and refurnishes her nest each spring, leaving the new houses for her more ambitious neighbors.

Of wood-warblers my territory affords many specimens. One spring a solitary Nashville warbler lingered near my cabin for a week. I heard his bright, ringing song at all hours of the day. The next spring there were two or more, and they nested in my pea-bushes. The black and white creeping warblers are perhaps the most abundant. A pair of them built a nest in a steep moss and lichen covered hillside, beside a high gray rock. Our path to Julian's Rock led just above it. It was an ideal spot and an ideal nest, but it came to grief. Some small creature sucked the eggs. On removing the nest I found an earth-stained egg beneath it. Evidently the egg had ripened before its receptacle was ready, and the mother, for good luck, had placed it in the foundation.

One day, as I sat at my table writing, I had a call from the worm-eating warbler. It came into the open door, flitted about inquisitively, and then, startled by the apparition at the table, dashed against the window-pane and fell down stunned. I picked it up, and it lay with closed eyes panting in my hand. I carried it into the open air. In a moment or two it opened its eyes, looked about, and then closed them and fell to panting again. Soon it looked up at me once more and about the room, and seemed to say: "Where am I? What has happened to me?" Presently the panting ceased, the bird's breathing became more normal, it gradually got its bearings, and, at a motion of my hand, darted away. This is an abundant warbler in my vicinity, and nested this year near by. I have discovered that it has an air-song — the song of ecstasy — like that of the oven-bird. I had long suspected it, as I frequently heard a fine burst of melody that was new to me. One June day I was fortunate enough to see the bird delivering its song in the air above the low trees. As with the oven-bird, its favorite hour is the early twilight, though I hear the song occasionally at other hours. The bird darts upward fifty feet or more, about half the height that the oven-bird attains, and gives forth a series of rapid, ringing musical notes, which quickly glide into the long, sparrow-like trill that forms its ordinary workaday song. While this part is being uttered, the singer is on its downward flight into the woods. The flight-song of the oven-bird is louder and more striking, and is not so shy and furtive a performance. The latter I hear many times every June twilight, and I frequently see the singer reach his climax a hundred feet or more in the air, and then mark his arrow-like flight downward. I have heard this song also in the middle of the night near my cabin. At such times it stands out on the stillness like a bursting rocket on the background of the night.

One or two mornings in April, at a very early hour, I am quite sure to hear the hermit thrush singing in the bushes near my window. How quickly I am transported to the Delectable Mountains and to the mossy solitudes of the northern woods! The winter wren also pauses briefly in his northern journey, and surprises and delights my ear with his sudden lyrical burst of melody. Such a dapper, fidgety, gesticulating, bobbing-up-and-down-and-out-and-in little bird, and yet full of such sweet, wild melody! To get him at his best, one needs to hear him in a dim, northern hemlock wood, where his voice reverberates as in a great hall; just as one should hear the veery in a beech and birch wood, beside a purling trout brook, when the evening shades are falling. It then becomes to you the voice of some particular spirit of the place and the hour. The veery does not inhabit the woods immediately about my cabin, but in the summer twilight he frequently comes up from the valley below and sings along the borders of my territory. How welcome his simple flute-like strain! The wood thrush is the leading chorister in the woods about me. He does not voice the wildness, but seems to give a touch of something half rural, half urban, — such is the power of association in bird-songs. In the evening twilight I often sit on the highest point of the rocky rim of the great granite bowl that holds my three acres of prairie soil, and see the shadows deepen, and listen to the bird voices that rise up from the forest below me. The songs of many wood thrushes make a sort of golden warp in the texture of sounds that is being woven about me. Now the flight-song of the oven-bird holds the ear, then the fainter one of the worm-eating warbler lures it. The carol of the robin, the vesper hymn of the tanager, the flute of the veery, are all on the air. Finally, as the shadows deepen and the stars begin to come out, the whip-poor-will suddenly strikes up. What a rude intrusion upon the serenity and harmony of the hour! A cry without music, insistent, reiterated, loud, penetrating, and yet the ear welcomes it also; the night and the solitude are so vast that they can stand it; and when, an hour later, as the night enters into full possession, the bird comes and serenades me under my window or upon my doorstep, my heart warms toward it. Its cry is a love-call, and there is something of the ardor and persistence of love in it, and when the female responds, and comes and hovers near, there is an interchange of subdued, caressing tones between the two birds that it is a delight to hear. During my first summer here one bird used to strike up every night from a high ledge of rocks in front of my door. At just such a moment in the twilight he would begin, the first to break the stillness. Then the others would follow, till the solitude was vocal with their calls. They are rarely heard later than ten o'clock. Then at day-break they take up the tale again, whipping poor Will till one pities him. One April morning between three and four o'clock, hearing one strike up near my window, I began counting its calls. My neighbor had told me he had heard one call over two hundred times without a break, which seemed to me a big story. But I have a much bigger one to tell. This bird actually laid upon the back of poor Will one thousand and eighty-eight blows, with only a barely perceptible pause here and there, as if to catch its breath. Then it stopped about half a minute and began again, uttering this time three hundred and ninety calls, when it paused, flew a little farther away, took up the tale once more, and continued till I fell asleep.

By day the whip-poor-will apparently sits motionless upon the ground. A few times in my walks through the woods I have started one up from almost under my feet. On such occasions the bird's movements suggest those of a bat; its wings make no noise, and it wavers about in an uncertain manner, and quickly drops to the ground again. One June day we flushed an old one with her two young, but there was no indecision or hesitation in the manner of the mother bird this time. The young were more than half fledged, and they scampered away a few yards and suddenly squatted upon the ground, where their protective coloring rendered them almost invisible. Then the anxious parent put forth all her arts to absorb our attention and lure us away from her offspring. She flitted before us from side to side, with spread wings and tail, now falling upon the ground, where she would remain a moment as if quite disabled, then perching upon an old stump or low branch with drooping, quivering wings, and imploring us by every gesture to take her and spare her young. My companion had his camera with him, but the bird would not remain long enough in one position for him to get her picture. The whip-poor-will builds no nest, but lays her two blunt, speckled eggs upon the dry leaves, where the plumage of the sitting bird blends perfectly with her surroundings. The eye, only a few feet away, has to search long and carefully to make her out. Every gray and brown and black tint of dry leaf and lichen, and bit of bark or broken twig, is copied in her plumage. In a day or two, after the young are hatched, the mother begins to move about with them through the woods.

When I want the wild of a little different flavor and quality from that immediately about my cabin, I go a mile through the woods to Black Creek, here called the Shattega, and put my canoe into a long, smooth, silent stretch of water that winds through a heavily timbered marsh till it leads into Black Pond, an oval sheet of water half a mile or more across. Here I get the moist, spongy, tranquil, luxurious side of Nature. Here she stands or sits knee-deep in water, and wreathes herself with pond-lilies in summer, and bedecks herself with scarlet maples in autumn. She is an Indian maiden, dark, subtle, dreaming, with glances now and then that thrill the wild blood in one's veins. The Shattega here is a stream without banks and with a just perceptible current. It is a waterway through a timbered marsh. The level floor of the woods ends in an irregular line where the level surface of the water begins. As one glides along in his boat, he sees various rank aquatic growths slowly waving in the shadowy depths beneath him. The larger trees on each side unite their branches above his head, so that at times he seems to be entering an arboreal cave out of which glides the stream. In the more open places the woods mirror themselves in the glassy surface till one seems floating between two worlds, clouds and sky and trees below him matching those around and above him. A bird flits from shore to shore, and one sees it duplicated against the sky in the under-world. What vistas open! What banks of drooping foliage, what grain and arch of gnarled branches, lure the eye as one drifts or silently paddles along! The stream has absorbed the shadows so long that it is itself like a liquid shadow. Its bed is lined with various dark vegetable growths, as with the skin of some huge, shaggy animal, the fur of which slowly stirs in the languid current. I go here in early spring, after the ice has broken up, to get a glimpse of the first wild ducks and to play the sportsman without a gun. I am sure I would not exchange the quiet surprise and pleasure I feel, as, on rounding some point or curve in the stream, two or more ducks spring suddenly out from some little cove or indentation in the shore, and with an alarum *quack, quack,* launch into the air and quickly gain the free spaces above the treetops, for the satisfaction of the gunner who

sees their dead bodies fall before his murderous fire.
He has only a dead duck, which, the chances are, he
will not find very toothsome at this season, while I
have a live duck with whistling wings cleaving the
air northward, where, in some lake or river of Maine
or Canada, in late summer, I may meet him again
with his brood. It is so easy, too, to bag the game
with your eye, while your gun may leave you only a
feather or two floating upon the water. The duck
has wit, and its wit is as quick as, or quicker than, the
sportsman's gun. One day in spring I saw a gunner
cut down a duck when it had gained an altitude of
thirty or forty feet above the stream. At the report
it stopped suddenly, turned a somersault, and fell
with a splash into the water. It fell like a brick, and
disappeared like one; only a feather and a few bub-
bles marked the spot where it struck. Had it sunk?
No; it had dived. It was probably winged, and in
the moment it occupied in falling to the water it had
decided what to do. It would go beneath the hunter,
since it could not escape above him; it could fly in
the water with only one wing, with its feet to aid it.
The gunner instantly set up a diligent search in all
directions, up and down along the shores, peering
long and intently into the depths, thrusting his oar
into the weeds and driftwood at the edge of the water, but no duck or sign of duck could he find. It
was as if the wounded bird had taken to the mimic
heaven that looked so sunny and real down there,

and gone on to Canada by that route. What astonished me was that the duck should have kept its presence of mind under such trying circumstances, and not have lost a fraction of a second of time in deciding on a course of action. The duck, I am convinced, has more sagacity than any other of our commoner fowl.

The day I see the first ducks I am pretty sure to come upon the first flock of blackbirds, — rusty grackles, — resting awhile on their northward journey amid the reeds, alders, and spice-bush beside the stream. They allow me to approach till I can see their yellow eyes and the brilliant iris on the necks and heads of the males. Many of them are vocal, and their united voices make a volume of sound that is analogous to a bundle of slivers. Sputtering, splintering, rasping, rending, their notes chafe and excite the ear. They suggest thorns and briers of sound, and yet are most welcome. What voice that rises from our woods or beside our waters in April is not tempered or attuned to the ear? Just as I like to chew the crinkleroot and the twigs of the spice-bush at this time, or at any time, for that matter, so I like to treat my ear to these more aspirated and astringent bird voices. Is it Thoreau who says they are like pepper and salt to this sense? In all the blackbirds we hear the voice of April not yet quite articulate; there is a suggestion of catarrh and influenza still in the air-passages. I should, perhaps, except the red-shouldered starling, whose clear and liquid *gur-ga-lee* or *o-ka-lee*, above the full water-courses, makes a different impression. The cowbird also has a clear note, but it seems to be wrenched or pumped up with much effort.

In May I go to Black Creek to hear the warblers and the water-thrushes. It is the only locality where I have ever heard the two water-thrushes, or accentors, singing at the same time,—the New York and the large-billed. The latter is much more abundant and much the finer songster. How he does make these watery solitudes ring with his sudden, brilliant burst of song! But the more northern species pleases the ear also with his quieter and less hurried strain. I drift in my boat and let the ear attend to the one, then to the other, while the eye takes note of their quick, nervous movements and darting flight. The smaller species probably does not nest along this stream, but the large-billed breeds here abundantly. The last nest I found was in the roots of an up-turned tree, with the water immediately beneath it. I had asked a neighboring farm-boy if he knew of any birds' nests.

"Yes," he said ; and he named over the nests of robins, highholes, sparrows, and others, and then that of a "tip-up."

At this last I pricked up my ears, so to speak. I had not seen a tip-up's nest in many a day. "Where?" I inquired.

"In the roots of a tree in the woods," said Charley.

"Not the nest of the 'tip-up,' or sandpiper," said I. "It builds on the ground in the open country near streams."

"Anyhow, it tipped," replied the boy.

He directed me to the spot, and I found, as I expected to find, the nest of the water-thrush. When the Vassar girls came again, I conducted them to the spot, and they took turns in walking a small tree trunk above the water, and gazing upon a nest brimming with the downy backs of young birds.

When I am listening to the water-thrushes, I am also noting with both eye and ear the warblers and vireos. There comes a week in May when the speckled Canada warblers are in the ascendant. They feed in the low bushes near the water's edge, and are very brisk and animated in voice and movement. The eye easily notes their slate-blue backs and yellow breasts with their broad band of black spots, and the ear quickly discriminates their not less marked and emphatic song.

In late summer I go to the Shattega, and to the lake out of which it flows, for white pond-lilies, and to feast my eye on the masses of purple loosestrife and the more brilliant but more hidden and retired cardinal-flower that bloom upon its banks. One cannot praise the pond-lily; his best words mar it, like the insects that eat its petals: but he can contemplate it as it opens in the morning sun and distills such perfume, such purity, such snow of petal and such gold of anther, from the dark water and still darker ooze. How feminine it seems beside its coarser and more robust congeners; how shy, how pliant, how fine in texture and star-like in form!

The loosestrife is a foreign plant, but it has made itself thoroughly at home here, and its masses of royal purple make the woods look civil and festive. The cardinal burns with a more intense fire, and fairly lights up the little dark nooks where it glasses itself in the still water. One must pause and look at it. Its intensity, its pure scarlet, the dark background upon which it is projected, its image in the still darker water, and its general air of retirement and seclusion, all arrest and delight the eye. It is a heart-throb of color on the bosom of the dark solitude.

The rarest and wildest animal that my neighborhood boasts of is the otter. Every winter we see the tracks of one or more of them upon the snow along Black Creek. But the eye that has seen the animal itself in recent years I cannot find. It probably makes its excursions along the creek by night. Follow its track — as large as that of a fair-sized dog — over the ice, and you will find that it ends at every open pool and rapid, and begins again upon the ice beyond. Sometimes it makes little excursions up the bank, its body often dragging in the snow like a log. My son followed the track one day far up the moun-

tain-side, where the absence of the snow caused him
to lose it. I like to think of so wild and shy a creature holding its own within sound of the locomo-
tive's whistle.

The fox passes my door in winter, and probably
in summer too, as do also the 'possum and the coon.
The latter tears down my sweet corn in the garden,
and the rabbit eats off my raspberry-bushes and nibbles my first strawberries, while the woodchucks eat
my celery and beans and peas. Chipmunks carry
off the corn I put out for the chickens, and weasels
eat the chickens themselves.

Many times during the season I have in my solitude a visit from a bald eagle. There is a dead tree
near the summit, where he often perches, and which
we call the " old eagle-tree." It is a pine, killed years
ago by a thunderbolt, — the bolt of Jove, — and
now the bird of Jove hovers about it or sits upon it.
I have little doubt that what attracted me to this
spot attracts him, — the seclusion, the savageness,
the elemental grandeur. Sometimes, as I look out of
my window early in the morning, I see the eagle
upon his perch, preening his plumage, or waiting for
the rising sun to gild the mountain-tops. When the
smoke begins to rise from my chimney, or he sees
me going to the spring for water, he concludes it is
time for him to be off. But he need not fear the
crack of the rifle here; nothing more deadly than
field-glasses shall be pointed at him while I am

about. Often in the course of the day I see him circling above my domain, or winging his way toward the mountains. His home is apparently in the Shawangunk Range, twenty or more miles distant, and I fancy he stops or lingers above me on his way to the river. The days on which I see him are not quite the same as the other days. I think my thoughts soar a little higher all the rest of the morning: I have had a visit from a messenger of Jove. The lift or range of those great wings has passed into my thought. I once heard a collector get up in a scientific body and tell how many eggs of the bald eagle he had clutched that season, how many from this nest, how many from that, and how one of the eagles had deported itself after he had killed its mate. I felt ashamed for him. He had only proved himself a superior human weasel. The man with the rifle and the man with the collector's craze are fast reducing the number of eagles in the country. Twenty years ago I used to see a dozen or more along the river in the spring when the ice was breaking up, where I now see only one or two, or none at all. In the present case, what would it profit me could I find and plunder my eagle's nest, or strip his skin from his dead carcass? Should I know him better? I do not want to know him that way. I want rather to feel the inspiration of his presence and noble bearing. I want my interest and sympathy to go with him in his continental voyaging up and down, and in his long, elevated flights to and from his eyrie upon the remote, solitary cliffs. He draws great lines across the sky ; he sees the forests like a carpet beneath him, he sees the hills and valleys as folds and wrinkles in a many-colored tapestry ; he sees the river as a silver belt connecting remote horizons. We climb mountain-peaks to get a glimpse of the spectacle that is hourly spread out beneath him. Dignity, elevation, repose, are his. I would have my thoughts take as wide a sweep. I would be as far removed from the petty cares and turmoils of this noisy and blustering world.

THE COMING OF SUMMER

WHO shall say when one season ends and another begins? Only the almanac-makers can fix these dates. It is like saying when babyhood ends and childhood begins, or when childhood ends and youth begins. To me spring begins when the catkins on the alders and the pussy-willows begin to swell; when the ice breaks up on the river and the first sea-gulls come prospecting northward. Whatever the date — the first or the middle or the last of March — when these signs appear, then I know spring is at hand. Her first birds — the bluebird, the song sparrow, the robin, the red-shouldered starling — are here or soon will be. The crows have a more confident caw, the sap begins to start in the sugar maple, the tiny boom of the first bee is heard, the downy woodpecker begins his resonant *tat, tat, tat,* on the dry limbs, and the cattle in the barnyard low long and loud with wistful looks toward the fields.

The first hint of summer comes when the trees are fully fledged and the nymph Shadow is born. See her cool circles again beneath the trees in the field, or her deeper and cooler retreats in the woods. On the slopes, on the opposite side of the river, there have been for months under the morning and noon sun only slight shadow tracings, a fretwork of shadow lines; but some morning in May I look across and see solid masses of shade falling from the trees athwart the sloping turf. How the eye revels in them! The trees are again clothed and in their right minds; myriad leaves rustle in promise of the coming festival. Now the trees are sentient beings; they have thoughts and fancies; they stir with emotion; they converse together; they whisper or dream in the twilight; they struggle and wrestle with the storm.

" Caught and curved by the gale,"

Tennyson says.

Summer always comes in the person of June, with a bunch of daisies on her breast and clover blossoms in her hands. A new chapter in the season is opened when these flowers appear. One says to himself, " Well, I have lived to see the daisies again and to smell the red clover." One plucks the first blossoms tenderly and caressingly. What memories are stirred in the mind by the fragrance of the one and the youthful face of the other! There is nothing else like that smell of the clover: it is the maidenly breath of summer; it suggests all fresh, buxom, rural things. A field of ruddy, blooming clover, dashed or sprinkled here and there with the snow-white of the daisies; its breath drifts into the road when you are passing; you hear the boom of bees, the voice of bobolinks, the twitter of swallows, the whistle of woodchucks; you smell wild strawberries; you see the cattle upon the hills; you see your youth, the youth of a happy farm-boy, rise before you. In Kentucky I once saw two fields, of one hundred acres each, all ruddy with blooming clover — perfume for a whole county.

The blooming orchards are the glory of May, the blooming clover-fields the distinction of June. Other characteristic June perfumes come from the honey-locusts and the blooming grapevines. At times and in certain localities the air at night and morning is heavy with the breath of the former, and along the lanes and roadsides we inhale the delicate fragrance of the wild grape. The early grasses, too, with their frostlike bloom, contribute something very welcome to the breath of June.

Nearly every season I note what I call the bridal day of summer — a white, lucid, shining day, with a delicate veil of mist softening all outlines. How the river dances and sparkles; how the new leaves of all the trees shine under the sun; the air has a soft lustre; there is a haze, it is not blue, but a kind of shining, diffused nimbus. No clouds, the sky a bluish white, very soft and delicate. It is the nuptial day of the season; the sun fairly takes the earth to be his own, for better or for worse, on such a day, and what marriages there are going on all about us: the marriages of the flowers, of the bees, of the birds. Everything suggests life, love, fruition. These bridal days are often repeated; the serenity and equipoise of the elements combine. They were such days as these that the poet Lowell had in mind when he exclaimed, "What is so rare as a day in June?" Here is the record of such a day, June 1, 1883: "Day perfect in temper, in mood, in everything. Foliage all out except on button-balls and celtis, and putting on its dark green summer color, solid shadows under the trees, and stretching down the slopes. A few indolent summer clouds here and there. A day of gently rustling and curtsying leaves, when the breeze almost seems to blow upward. The fields of full-grown, nodding rye slowly stir and sway like vast assemblages of people. How the chimney swallows chipper as they sweep past! The vireo's cheerful warble echoes in the leafy maples; the branches of the Norway spruce and the hemlocks have gotten themselves new light green tips; the dandelion's spheres of ethereal down rise above the grass: and now and then one of them suddenly goes down: the little chippy, or social sparrow, has thrown itself upon the frail stalk and brought it to the ground, to feed upon its seeds; here it gets the first fruits of the season. The first red and white clover heads have just opened, the yellow rock-rose and the sweet viburnum are in bloom; the bird chorus is still full and animated; the keys of the red maple strew the ground, and the cotton of the early everlasting drifts upon the air." For several days there was but little change. "Getting toward the high tide of summer. The air well warmed up, Nature in her jocund mood, still, all leaf and sap. The days are idyllic. I lie on my back on the grass in the shade of the house, and look up to the soft, slowly moving clouds, and to the chimney swallows disporting themselves up there in the breezy depths. No hardening in vegetation yet. The moist, hot, fragrant breath of the fields — mingled odor of blossoming grasses, clover, daisies, rye — the locust blossoms, dropping. What a humming about the hives; what freshness in the shade of every tree; what contentment in the flocks and herds! The springs are yet full and cold; the shaded watercourses and pond margins begin to draw one." Go to the top of the hill on such a morning, say by nine o'clock, and see how unspeakably fresh and full the world looks. The morning shadows yet linger everywhere, even in the sunshine; a kind of blue coolness and freshness, the vapor of dew tinting the air.

Heat and moisture, the father and mother of all that lives, when June has plenty of these, the increase is sure.

Early in June the rye and wheat heads begin to

nod; the motionless stalks have a reflective, meditative air. A little while ago, when their heads were
empty or filled only with chaff and sap, how straight
up they held them! Now that the grain is forming,
they have a sober, thoughtful look. It is one of the
most pleasing spectacles of June, a field of rye
gently shaken by the wind. How the breezes are
defined upon its surface — a surface as sensitive
as that of water; how they trip along, little breezes
and big breezes together! Just as this glaucous
green surface of the rye-field bends beneath the light
tread of the winds, so, we are told, the crust of the
earth itself bends beneath the giant strides of the
great atmospheric waves.

There is one bird I seldom hear till June, and that
is the cuckoo. Sometimes the last days of May
bring him, but oftener it is June before I hear his
note. The cuckoo is the true recluse among our
birds. I doubt if there is any joy in his soul. " Rain-
crow," he is called in some parts of the country.
His call is supposed to bode rain. Why do other
birds, the robin for instance, often make war upon
the cuckoo, chasing it from the vicinity of their
nests? There seems to be something about the
cuckoo that makes its position among the birds
rather anomalous. Is it at times a parasitical bird,
dropping its eggs into other birds' nests? Or is
there some suggestion of the hawk about our species
as well as about the European? I do not know. I

only know that it seems to be regarded with a suspicious eye by other birds, and that it wanders about at night in a way that no respectable bird should. The birds that come in March, as the bluebird, the robin, the song sparrow, the starling, build in April; the April birds, such as the brown thrasher, the barn swallow, the chewink, the water-thrush, the oven-bird, the chippy, the high-hole, the meadowlark, build in May, while the May birds, the kingbird, the wood thrush, the oriole, the orchard starling, and the warblers, build in June. The April nests are exposed to the most dangers: the storms, the crows, the squirrels, are all liable to cut them off. The midsummer nests, like that of the goldfinch and the waxwing, or cedar-bird, are the safest of all.

In March the door of the seasons first stands ajar a little; in April it is opened much wider; in May the windows go up also; and in June the walls are fairly taken down and the genial currents have free play everywhere. The event of March in the country is the first good sap day, when the maples thrill with the kindling warmth; the event of April is the new furrow and the first seeding; — how ruddy and warm the soil looks just opened to the sun! — the event of May is the week of orchard bloom; with what sweet, pensive gladness one walks beneath the pink-white masses, while long, long thoughts descend upon him! See the impetuous orioles chase one another amid the branches, shaking down the fragrant snow. Here the rose-breasted grosbeak is in the blooming cherry tree, snipping off the blossoms with that heavy beak of his — a spot of crimson and black half hidden in masses of white petals. This orchard bloom travels like a wave. In March it is in the Carolinas; by the middle of April its crest has reached the Potomac; a week or ten days later it is in New Jersey; then in May it sweeps through New York and New England; and early in June it is breaking upon the orchards in Canada. Finally, the event of June is the fields ruddy with clover and milk-white with daisies.

DEVIOUS PATHS

THERE is no better type or epitome of wild nature than the bird's-nest — something built, and yet as if it grew, a part of the ground, or of the rock, or of the branch upon which it is placed; beginning so coarsely, so irregularly, and ending so finely and symmetrically; so unlike the work of hands, and yet the result of a skill beyond hands; and when it holds its complement of eggs, how pleasing, how suggestive!

The bird adapts means to an end, and yet so differently from the way of man, — an end of which it does not know the value or the purpose. We know it is prompted to it by the instinct of reproduction. When the woodpecker in the fall excavates a lodge in a dry limb, we know he is prompted to it by the instinct of self-preservation, but the birds themselves obey the behests of nature without knowledge.

A bird's-nest suggests design, and yet it seems almost haphazard; the result of a kind of madness, yet with method in it. The hole the woodpecker drills for its cell is to the eye a perfect circle, and the rim of most nests is as true as that of a cup. The circle and the sphere exist in nature; they are mother forms and hold all other forms. They are easily attained; they are spontaneous and inevitable. The bird models her nest about her own breast ; she turns round and round in it, and its circular character results as a matter of course. Angles, right lines, measured precision, so characteristic of the works of man, are rarely met with in organic nature.

Nature reaches her ends by devious paths; she loiters, she meanders, she plays by the way; she surely " arrives," but it is always in a blind, hesitating, experimental kind of fashion. Follow the tunnels of the ants or the crickets, or of the moles and the weasels, underground, or the courses of the streams or the paths of the animals above ground — how they turn and hesitate, how wayward and undecided they are! A right line seems out of the question.

The oriole often weaves strings into her nest ; sometimes she binds and overhands the part of the rim where she alights in going in, to make it stronger, but it is always done in a hit-or-miss, childish sort of way, as one would expect it to be; the strings are massed, or snarled, or left dangling at loose ends, or are caught around branches; the weaving and the sewing are effective, and the whole nest is a marvel of blind skill, of untaught intelligence; yet how unmethodical, how delightfully irregular, how unmistakably a piece of wild nature!

Sometimes the instinct of the bird is tardy, and the egg of the bird gets ripe before the nest is ready; in such a case the egg is of course lost. I once found the nest of the black and white creeping warbler in a mossy bank in the woods, and under the nest was an egg of the bird. The warbler had excavated the site for her nest, dropped her egg into it, and then gone on with her building. Instinct is not always inerrant. Nature is wasteful, and plays the game with a free hand. Yet what she loses on one side she gains on another; she is like that least bittern Mr. Frank M. Chapman tells about. Two of the bittern's five eggs had been punctured by the long-billed marsh wren. When the bird returned to her nest and found the two eggs punctured, she made no outcry, showed no emotion, but deliberately proceeded to eat them. Having done this, she dropped the empty shells over the side of the nest, together with any straws that had become soiled in the process, cleaned her bill, and proceeded with her incubation. This was Nature in a nut-shell, — or rather egg-shell, — turning her mishaps to some good account. If the egg will not make a bird, it will make food; if not food, then fertilizer.

Among nearly all our birds, the female is the active business member of the partnership; she has a turn for practical affairs; she chooses the site of the nest, and usually builds it unaided. The life of the male is more or less a holiday or picnic till the young are hatched, when his real cares begin, for he does his part in feeding them. One may see the male cedar-bird attending the female as she is busy with her nest-building, but never, so far as I have observed, assisting her. One spring I observed with much interest a phœbe-bird building her nest not far from my cabin in the woods. The male looked on approvingly, but did not help. He perched most of the time on a mullein stalk near the little spring run where Phœbe came for mud. In the early morning hours she made her trips at intervals of a minute or two. The male flirted his tail and called encouragingly, and when she started up the hill with her load he would accompany her part way, to help her over the steepest part, as it were, then return to his perch and watch and call for her return. For an hour or more I witnessed this little play in bird life, in which the female's part was so primary and the male's so secondary. There is something in such things that seems to lend support to Professor Lester F. Ward's contention, as set forth in his "Pure Sociology," that in the natural evolution of the two sexes the female was first and the male second ; that he was made from her rib, so to speak, and not she from his.

With our phalarope and a few Australian birds, the position of the two sexes as indicated above

A Wood Thrush

is reversed, the females having the ornaments and bright colors and doing the courting, while the male does the incubating. In a few cases also the female is much the more masculine, noisy, and pugnacious. With some of our common birds, such as the woodpeckers, the chickadee, and the swallows, both sexes take part in nest-building.

It is a very pretty sight to witness a pair of wood thrushes building their nest. Indeed, what is there about the wood thrush that is not pleasing? He is a kind of visible embodied melody. Some birds are so sharp and nervous and emphatic in their movements, as the common snowbird or junco, the flashing of whose white tail quills expresses the character of the bird. But all the ways of the wood thrush are smooth and gentle, and suggest the melody of its song. It is the only bird thief I love to see carrying off my cherries. It usually takes only those dropped upon the ground by other birds, and with the red or golden globe impaled upon its beak, its flight across the lawn is a picture delightful to behold. One season a pair of them built a nest in a near-by grove; morning after morning, for many mornings, I used to see the two going to and from the nest, over my vineyard and currant patch and pear orchard, in quest of, or bringing material for, the structure. They flew low, the female in the lead, the male just behind in line with her, timing his motions to hers, the two making a brown, gently undulating line, very pretty to look upon, from my neighbor's field where they obtained the material, to the tree that held the nest. A gentle, gliding flight, hurried but hushed, as it were, and expressive of privacy and loving preoccupation. The male carried no material; apparently he was simply the escort of his mate; but he had an air of keen and joyous interest. He never failed to attend her each way, keeping about a yard behind her, and flying as if her thought were his thought and her wish his wish. I have rarely seen anything so pretty in bird life. The movements of all our thrushes except the robin give one this same sense of harmony, — nothing sharp or angular or abrupt. Their gestures are as pleasing as their notes.

One evening, while seated upon my porch, I had convincing proof that musical or song contests do take place among the birds. Two wood thrushes who had nests near by sat on the top of a dead tree and pitted themselves against each other in song for over half an hour, contending like champions in a game, and certainly affording the rarest treat in wood thrush melody I had ever had. They sang and sang with unwearied spirit and persistence, now and then changing position or facing in another direction, but keeping within a few feet of each other. The rivalry became so obvious and was so interesting that I finally made it a point not to take my eyes from the singers. The twilight deepened till their forms began to grow dim; then one of the birds could stand the strain no longer, the limit of fair competition had been reached, and seeming to say, "I will silence you, anyhow," it made a spiteful dive at its rival, and in hot pursuit the two disappeared in the bushes beneath the tree. Of course I would not say that the birds were consciously striving to outdo each other in song ; it was the old feud between males in the love season, not a war of words or of blows, but of song. Had the birds been birds of brilliant plumage, the rivalry would probably have taken the form of strutting and showing off their bright colors and ornaments.

An English writer on birds, Edmund Selous, describes a similar song contest between two nightingales. "Jealousy," he says, "did not seem to blind them to the merit of each other's performance. Though often one, upon hearing the sweet, hostile strains, would burst forth instantly itself, — and here there was no certain mark of appreciation, — yet sometimes, perhaps quite as often, it would put its head on one side and listen with exactly the appearance of a musical connoisseur, weighing, testing, and appraising each note as it issued from the rival bill. A curious, half-suppressed expression would steal, or seem to steal (for Fancy may play her part in such matters), over the listening bird, and the idea appear to be, 'How exquisite would be those strains were they not sung by ——, and yet I must admit that they are exquisite.'" Fancy no doubt does play a part in such matters. It may well be doubted if birds are musical connoisseurs, or have anything like human appreciation of their own or of each other's songs. My reason for thinking so is this: I have heard a bobolink with an instrument so defective that its song was broken and inarticulate in parts, and yet it sang with as much apparent joy and abandon as any of its fellows. I have also heard a hermit thrush with a similar defect or impediment that appeared to sing entirely to its own satisfaction. It would be very interesting to know if these poor singers found mates as readily as their more gifted brothers. If they did, the Darwinian theory of "sexual selection" in such matters, according to which the finer songster would carry off the female, would fall to the ground. Yet it is certain that it is during the mating and breeding season that these "song combats" occur, and the favor of the female would seem to be the matter in dispute. Whether or not it be expressive of actual jealousy or rivalry, we have no other words to apply to it.

A good deal of light is thrown upon the ways of nature as seen in the lives of our solitary wasps, so skillfully and charmingly depicted by George W. Peckham and his wife in their work on those insects. So whimsical, so fickle, so forgetful, so fussy, so wise, and yet so foolish, as these little people are! such victims of routine and yet so individual, such apparent foresight and yet such thoughtlessness, at such great pains and labor to dig a hole and build a cell, and then at times sealing it up without storing it with food or laying the egg, half finishing hole after hole, and then abandoning them without any apparent reason; sometimes killing their spiders, at other times only paralyzing them; one species digging its burrow before it captures its game, others capturing the game and then digging the hole ; some of them hanging the spider up in the fork of a weed to keep it away from the ants while they work at their nest, and running to it every few minutes to see that it is safe; others laying the insect on the ground while they dig; one species walking backward and dragging its spider after it, and when the spider is so small that it carries it in its mandible, still walking backward as if dragging it, when it would be much more convenient to walk forward. A curious little people, leading their solitary lives and greatly differentiated by the solitude, hardly any two alike, one nervous and excitable, another calm and unhurried; one careless in her work, another neat and thorough; this one suspicious, that one confiding ; Ammophila using a pebble to pack down the earth in her burrow, while another species uses the end of her abdomen, — verily a queer little people, with a lot of wild nature about them, and a lot of human nature, too.

I think one can see how this development of individuality among the solitary wasps comes about. May it not be because the wasps are solitary? They live alone. They have no one to imitate; they are uninfluenced by their fellows. No community interests override or check individual whims or peculiarities. The innate tendency to variation, active in all forms of life, has with them full sway. Among the social bees or wasps one would not expect to find those differences between individuals. The members of a colony all appear alike in habits and in dispositions. Colonies differ, as every bee-keeper knows, but probably the members composing it differ very little. The community interests shape all alike. Is it not the same in a degree among men? Does not solitude bring out a man's peculiarities and differentiate him from others? The more one lives alone, the more he becomes unlike his fellows. Hence the original and racy flavor of woodsmen, pioneers, lone dwellers in Nature's solitudes. Thus isolated communities develop characteristics of their own. Constant intercommunication, the friction of travel, of streets, of books, of newspapers, make us all alike; we are, as it were, all pebbles upon the same shore, washed by the same waves.

Among the larger of vertebrate animals, I think, one might reasonably expect to find more individuality among those that are solitary than among those that are gregarious; more among birds of prey than among water-fowl, more among foxes than among prairie-dogs, more among moose than among sheep or buffalo, more among grouse than among quail. But I do not know that this is true.

Yet among none of these would one expect to find the diversity of individual types that one finds among men. No two dogs of the same breed will be found to differ as two men of the same family often differ. An original fox, or wolf, or bear, or beaver, or crow, or crab, — that is, one not merely different from his fellows, but obviously superior to them, differing from them as a master mind differs from the ordinary mind, — I think, one need not expect to find. It is quite legitimate for the animal-story writer to make the most of the individual differences in habits and disposition among the animals; he has the same latitude any other story writer has, but he is bound also by the same law of probability, the same need of fidelity to nature. If he proceed upon the theory that the wild creatures have as pronounced individuality as men have, that there are master minds among them, inventors and discoverers of new ways, born captains and heroes, he will surely "o'erstep the modesty of nature."

The great diversity of character and capacity among men doubtless arises from their greater and more complex needs, relations, and aspirations. The animals' needs in comparison are few, their relations simple, and their aspirations *nil*. One cannot see what could give rise to the individual types and exceptional endowments that are often claimed for them. The law of variation, as I have said, would give rise to differences, but not to a sudden reversal of race habits, or to animal geniuses.

The law of variation is everywhere operative — less so now, no doubt, than in the earlier history of organic life on the globe. Yet Nature is still experimenting in her blind way, and hits upon many curious differences and departures. But I suppose if the race of man were exterminated, man would never arise again. I doubt if the law of evolution could ever again produce him, or any other species of animal.

This principle of variation was no doubt much more active back in geologic time, during the early history of animal life upon the globe, than it is in this late age. And for the reason that animal life was less adapted to its environment than it is now, the struggle for life was sharper. Perfect adaptation of any form of life to the conditions surrounding it seems to check variability. Animal and plant life seem to vary more in this country than in England because the conditions of life are harder. The extremes of heat and cold, of wet and dry, are much greater. It has been found that the eggs of the English sparrow vary in form and color more in the United States than in Great Britain. Certain American shells are said to be more variable than the English. Among our own birds it has been found that the "migratory species evince a greater amount of individual variation than do non-migrating species" because they are subject to more varying conditions of food and climate. I think we may say, then, if there were no struggle for life, if uniformity of temperature and means of subsistence everywhere prevailed, there would be little or no variation and no new species would arise. The causes of variation seem to be the inequality and imperfection of things; the pressure of life is unequally distributed, and this is one of Nature's ways that accounts for much that we see about us.

TWO BIRDS'-NESTS

I CONSIDER myself lucky if, in the course of a season, I can pick up two or three facts in natural history that are new to me. To have a new delight in an old or familiar fact is not always easy, and is perhaps quite as much to be desired. The familiar we always have with us; to see it with fresh eyes so as to find a new pleasure in it,—that is a great point.

I think one never sees a bird's-nest of any kind without fresh pleasure. It is such a charming secret, and is usually so well kept by the tree, or bank, or bit of ground that holds it; and then it is such a dainty and exquisite cradle or nursery amid its rough and wild surroundings, — a point so cherished and cared for in the apparently heedless economy of the fields or woods!

When it is a new nest and one long searched for, the pleasure is of course proportionally greater. Such a pleasure came to me one day last summer in early July, when I discovered the nest of the water-thrush or water-wagtail.

The nest of its cousin the oven-bird, called by the

old ornithologists the golden-crowned thrush, was familiar to me, as it probably is to most country boys, — a nest partly thrust under the dry leaves upon the ground in the woods, and holding four or five whitish eggs covered with reddish-brown spots. The mother bird is in size less than the sparrow, and in color is a light olive with a speckled breast, and she is the prettiest walker to be seen in the woods.

The water-accentor or wagtail is a much rarer bird, and of a darker olive green. As the color of the oven-bird harmonizes with the dry leaves over which it walks, so the color of the wagtail is in keeping with the dark-veined brooks and forest pools along which it flits and near which it nests.

With me it is an April bird. When the spice-bush is in bloom along the fringes of the creeks, and the leaves of the adder's-tongue or fawn lily have pierced the mould, I expect to hear the water-thrush. Its song is abrupt, bright, and ringing. It contrasts with its surroundings as does the flower of the blood-root which you may have seen that day.

It is the large-billed or Louisiana water-thrush of which I am speaking. The other species, the New York water-accentor, is rarer with me, and goes farther into the mountains.

The large-billed is a quick, shy, emphatic bird in its manner. Some birds, such as the true thrushes, impress one as being of a serene, contemplative disposition; there is a kind of harmony and tranquillity in all their movements; but the bird I am speaking of is sharp, restless, hurried. Its song is brilliant, its movements quick and decisive. You hear its emphatic chirp, and see it dart swiftly beneath or through the branches that reach out over the creek.

It nests upon the ground, or amid the roots of an upturned tree in the woods near the water that it haunts. Every season for many years I have looked for the nest, but failed to find it till last summer.

My son and I were camping in the Catskills, when one day, as I was slowly making my way down one of those limpid trout streams, I saw a water-thrush dart from out a pile of logs and driftwood that the floods had left on the margin of the stream. The bird at once betrayed much anxiety, and I knew the nest was near.

I proceeded carefully to explore the pile of driftwood, and especially the roots of an upturned tree which it held. I went over the mass almost inch by inch several times. There was a little cavern in it, a yard or more deep, where the light was dim; a translucent pool of water formed the floor of it, and kept me from passing its threshold. I suspected the nest was in there amid the roots or broken branches, but my eye failed to detect it.

"I will go on with my fishing," I said, "and return to-morrow and lay siege to this secret."

So on the morrow I returned, and carefully se-
creted myself on a mossy bank a few yards from the
pile of driftwood. Presently the parent bird came
with food in its beak, but instantly spying me, though
I fancied that in my recumbent position and faded
gray clothes I simulated well an old log, she grew
alarmed and refused to approach the nest.

She flitted nervously about from point to point,
her attention directed to me, and uttering a sharp,
chiding note. Soon her mate came, and the two birds
flitted about me, peering, attitudinizing, scolding.
The mother bird is always the bolder and more
demonstrative on such occasions. I was amused at
her arts and feints and her sudden fits of alarm.
Sometimes she would quickly become silent, and
stealthily approach the entrance of the little cavern
in the pile of driftwood; then, her fears and suspicions reviving, with emphatic chirps she would try
again to penetrate the mystery of that motionless,
prostrate form on the bank.

The dead branch of a tree that slanted down to
the bed of the stream near me was her favorite perch.
Inch by inch she would hop up it, her body moving like a bandmaster's baton, her notes sharp and
emphatic, her wings slightly drooping, meanwhile
bringing first one eye and then the other to bear
upon the supposed danger.

While she was thus engaging my attention, I
saw the male quickly slip into the little cavern with

loaded beak, and in a moment reappear. He ran swiftly along the dry pebbles a few yards, and then took to wing, and joined in the cry against me. In a few moments he disappeared, presumably in quest of more food.

The mother, after many feints and passes and false moves, half-fearful of her own rashness, darted into the little cavern also. She soon shot out from it on nimble foot, as had her mate, then took to wing, and to fresh peering and abuse of the strange object on the bank.

The male was soon on the scene again, and after a little flourishing, entered the shadow of the cavern as before. Pausing a moment, the female did the same.

Evidently their suspicions were beginning to be lulled. They had seen fishermen many, a few every day for weeks, and had grown used to them; these had gone on about their business ; but this one that tarried and seemed bent on finding out other people's business, — here was cause for alarm!

In less than half an hour I felt sure I had the birds' secret, — I had seen in the recesses of the cavern the exact spot where they seemed to pause a moment and then turn back. So I approached the spot confidently ; I got down on my knees and charged my eyes to find the nest.

I am surprised that they seem baffled. At the particular niche or shelf in the mass of roots they report only moss or moist stones, — no nest there. I peer long and long. The little pool of limpid water keeps me five or six feet away.

Well, there must be some unseen hole or cavity in there which leads to the nest beyond the reach of the eye. But I will watch again and be sure. So I retreat to the bank, and the same little comedy or drama is played as before.

At last I am positive I can put my hand upon the nest. I procure a fragment of a board, bridge over the little pool, thrust my head into the dim light of the cavity, and closely scan every inch of the surface. No nest, says the eye. Then I will try another sense; I will feel with my hand.

Slowly my hand explores the place; presently it touches something soft and warm at the very spot where I had seen the birds pause. It is the backs of the young birds; they have flattened themselves down until their beaks are on a level with the top of the nest. They have baffled the eye because, in the scant light, they blend perfectly with their surroundings and just fill the depression of the nest. The hand, going behind form and color, finds them out. I felt that I had penetrated one of the prettiest secrets in all the woods, and got a new glimpse of the art and cunning of a bird.

The young were between down and feather, of a grayish slate color, and they played their part well. At my approach they would settle down in the nest till, instead of five, they became one, and that one a circular mass of dark bluish stone or fragment of bark. When I withdrew or concealed myself, they would rise up and their individual forms become outlined.

Another new nest which it was my luck to find the past summer was that of the worm-eating warbler, a bird of the Carolinian fauna, that heretofore has not been known to breed in our State — New York. It was a new find, then, in a double sense, new to me and new to the ornithology of the State.

One day in early June, as I was walking along a path on the side of a bushy hill, near dense woods, I had a glimpse of a small brown bird that dashed away from the bank but a few feet from me. I took it to be the oven-bird.

Looking to the spot from whence it started, I saw a bird with a striped head standing on the edge of a nest in the side of the shelving bank, with something white in its beak. I saw the heads of the young birds beneath, and took in the situation instantly; I had surprised the mother bird while she was waiting upon her young. She stood motionless, half-turned toward me, still keeping the white mass in her beak.

Neither of us stirred for a minute or two, and the other parent made no sound, though he lingered but a few yards away.

Presently I slowly withdrew, and sat down a few paces away. The male bird now became quite un-

easy, and flitted from bush to bush and uttered his
alarm chirp. The mother bird never stirred. I could
see her loaded beak from where I sat. In two or
three minutes she dropped or otherwise disposed of
her morsel, but kept her place above her young.
Then her mate, taking his cue from her, quieted
down and soon disappeared from view.

After long waiting I approached the nest, and
pausing ten feet away, regarded it some moments.
The bird never stirred. Then I came nearer, and
when I sat down within four or five feet of the nest,
the bird flew out upon the ground before me, and
sought to lure me away by practicing the old confi-
dence game that birds so often resort to on such
occasions.

She was seized with incipient paralysis in her
members; she dragged herself about upon the
ground; she quivered and tottered and panted with
open beak, and seemed on the point of going all to
pieces. Seeing this game did not work and that I
remained unmoved, she suddenly changed her tactics; she flew up to a limb and gave me a piece of her
mind in no equivocal terms. This brought the male,
and true to his name, he had a worm in his beak.

Both now joined in the scolding, and the rumpus
attracted a vireo to the spot, who came to see what
the danger really was. But evidently the warblers
regarded his presence as an intrusion.

The nest was in the edge of the bank where the

soil was broken away a little, and was mainly composed of dry leaves and pine needles. The young, five in number, were probably a week old.

I came again the next day, and found the bird sitting on the edge of the nest as before, and ready, when I disturbed her, with the same arts to lure me away. I paid frequent visits to the place thereafter till the young had flown.

The song of the male — a little shuffling chant much like that of Chippy — was frequently heard. This warbler may be instantly known by its olivaceous color and the four sharp black stripes on its buff-colored head. It is one of the prettiest and most interesting of the warblers.

FUSS AND FEATHERS

PROBABLY we have no other familiar bird keyed up to the same degree of intensity as the house wren. He seems to be the one bird whose cup of life is always overflowing. The wren is habitually in an ecstasy either of delight or of rage. He probably gets on the nerves of more persons than any other of our birds. He is so shrilly and overflowingly joyous, or else so sharply and harshly angry and pugnacious — a lyrical burst one minute, and a volley of chiding, staccato notes the next. More restless than the wind, he is a tiny dynamo of bird energy. From his appearance in May till his last brood is out in midsummer, he repeats his shrill, hurried little strain about ten times a minute for about ten hours a day, and cackles and chatters between-times. He expends enough energy in giving expression to his happiness, or vent to his anger, in the course of each day to carry him halfway to the Gulf. He sputters, he chatters, he carols; he excites the wrath of bluebirds, phœbes, orioles, robins; he darts into holes; he bobs up in unexpected places; he nests in old hats, in dinner-pails, in pumps, in old shoes. Give him a twig and a feather and a hole in almost anything, and his cup is full. How absurdly happy he is over a few dry twigs there in that box, and his little freckled mate sitting upon her eggs! His throat swells and throbs as if he had all the winds of Æolus imprisoned in it, and the little tempest of joy in there rages all the time. His song goes off as suddenly as if some one had touched a spring or switched on a current. If feathers can have a feathered edge, the wren has it.

"What bird is that?" asked an invalid wife, seated on the porch near a wren-box. "Is it never still, and never silent? It gets on my nerves."

"Neither still nor silent long at a time," replied her husband, "except when asleep."

It repeats its song at least six thousand times a day for two or three months, at the same time that it brings many scores of insects to feed its young. But this activity does not use up all the energy of the wren. He gets rid of some of the surplus in building cock, or sham, nests in every unoccupied bird-box near him. He fills the cavities up with twigs, and I have even seen him carry food into these sham nests, playing that he had young there. (I saw him do it yesterday, July 7th; he held in his beak what seemed to be a small green worm.) Not even these activities use up all his energy; it overflows in his shaking and vibrating wings while in song.

The song of the house wren is rather harsh and shrill, far inferior as a musical performance to that of the winter wren. The songs of the two differ as their nests differ, or as soft green moss and feathers differ from dry twigs and a little dry grass. A truly sylvan strain is that of the winter wren, suggesting deep wildwood solitudes, while that of the house wren is more in keeping with the noise and clatter of the farm and dooryard. He begins singing by or before four o'clock in the morning, and for the first hour hardly stops to take breath, and all the forenoon the pauses between his volleys of notes are of but a few seconds.

I find that there are good bird-observers who accuse the wren of destroying the eggs of other birds. I have no first-hand evidence that such is a fact, but the hostility of several other species of birds toward the wren gives color to the charge. Why, for instance, should the phœbe-bird make a savage drive at him, if she has not some old score of that kind to wipe out? or the song sparrow chase him into a vine or a bush and keep him a prisoner there for a few moments, as I have seen him do?

As I was sitting on the platform of the fruit-house one morning, watching the wood thrushes at nest-building, there was a rustle of wings almost at my elbow, and the snapping of a phœbe's beak. I turned in time to see a brown speck darting under the floor, and a phœbe-bird close on to its heels. The speck was a wren, and the phœbe was driving for it viciously. How spitefully her beak did snap! As the wren eluded her, phœbe turned quickly and disappeared down the hill, where she had a nest on a rafter in the lower fruit-house.

This season there are four wrens' nests about my place, in hollow limbs and boxes which we have put up, and three bluebirds' nests. The wrens and the bluebirds often come into collision; mainly, I think, because they are rivals for the same nesting-sites. The bluebird, with all his soft, plaintive notes, has a marked vein of pugnacity in him, and is at times a lively "scrapper"; and the wren is no "peace-at-any-price bird, and will stand up for his rights very bravely against his big blue-coated rival.

Late one afternoon, when I was busy in the garden near the end of the vineyard, where there was a bird-box, I suddenly heard the loud, emphatic note of a bluebird mingled with the chiding cackle and chatter of a house wren. I saw the bluebird dive savagely at the wren and drive him into a currant-bush, where he would scold and "sass back," and then break out into a shrill, brief song. Presently a female oriole came and joined the bluebird in persecuting the wren, which answered back from its safe retreat in the bushes with harsh chatter and snatches of tantalizing song. The bluebird took up his stand on the grape-post that supported the bird-box in which the wren had a nest, and from this outlook he grew eloquent in his denunciation of wrens. His loud, rapid voice and the answering cackle of the wren attracted the attention of their

Least Flycatcher

bird neighbors. Four robins came, one after another, and perched on the tops of surrounding posts, silent but interested spectators. A male oriole came, a catbird came, two song sparrows came, and then a male goldfinch perched near by. The birds were evidently curious to know what all this loud altercation was about — very human in this respect.

After the bluebird had eased his mind a little about wrens, he dropped down to the box, and, clinging to the entrance of the nest, looked in. Instantly the wren was on his back, scolding excitedly. The bluebird turned to seize him, but was not quick enough, and there was a brown streak, with a blue streak close behind it, to the nearest currant-bush, in which the wren again chattered and sang in derision. The bluebird again resumed his perch above the nest and was louder and more emphatic than ever in his protests. It was really very amusing to see the bluebird stand up so straight there on the post, like a stump orator, delivering his philippic against the wren. His whole bearing and tone expressed indignation and an outraged sense of justice. I fancied him saying: "My friends and neighbors, I want to bear witness before you of the despicable character of this chattering, skulking, impudent house wren. He is an intolerable nuisance. He crosses my path daily. Every honest bird hates him. He fills up the boxes he cannot occupy with his rubbish, and assaults me if I look into them and criticize his conduct. He is sly and meddlesome, and a disturber of the peace. He has the manners of a blackguard and the habits of a thief and a despoiler. His throat and tongue are brass, and his song is as harsh as the dry twigs he makes his nest of. I ask you to join me in putting him down." His audience listened and looked on with interest, I will not say with amusement. The humor of the situation probably appealed to me alone. The birds were only anxious to find out if a possible common danger threatened them all. But to me the situation had an element of comedy in it, and made me laugh in spite of myself.

Again the bluebird essayed to look into that hole, and as quick as a flash the wren was on his back. Whether or not he used his sharp beak, I could not tell, as the assailed turned upon his assailant so quickly — but not quick enough to get in a counter-stroke. The vines and bushes were again a house of safety for the wren. Three or four times the bluebird asserted his natural right to look into any hole or cavity he had a mind to, and each time the wren denied that right in the way I have described. But such jangles among the birds are usually brief. One by one the spectators flew away; and finally the chief actor in the little drama flew away, and the wren warbled in a strain of triumph.

The next day I discovered that the wren had only begun building a nest in the box, probably a cock nest. One thing arrested my attention; the box had a big crack in it from the entrance nearly to the bottom. This crack the wren had evidently essayed to stop with twigs. At first sight my impression was that the twigs had accidentally got caught in the crack in the bird's effort to get them into the nest. But, after carefully considering the matter, I see I must credit him with a purpose to mend his house. He had first put two small twigs into the crack and then finished the job with a much larger twig, eight inches long, which closed the opening very effectually. This last twig was larger and longer than wrens ever use in their nests. It was a very clever stroke.

I think the male wrens have sham battles as well as sham nests; they must work off their superfluous animation in some way. For hours one early July afternoon two males, one of whom had a cock nest a few yards below me in a box on a grape-post, and the other a few yards above me in a box on the corner of the veranda, amused and delayed me in my eager reading of the war news (the British had just begun their great offensive in France) by engaging in what appeared to be a most determined song contest from their respective perches a few yards apart. How their throats were convulsed! Under what pressure of jealousy or rivalry they did hurl shrill defiance at each other in that, to me, languid summer afternoon! Back and forth, back and forth, went the voluble challenges, the birds facing each other with drooping wings and throbbing breasts. The grape-post wren seemed to be in the more aggressive mood. When he could stand it no longer, he would dart up the hill at his opponent on the low branch of a maple, who never stood to his guns, and the two would make a brown streak in a wide circle around the maples and the Study, and down the hill round the summer-house, keeping just so far apart, and never actually coming to blows. Then they would take up their old positions and renew the vocal contest with the same spirit as before, till one of them was again carried off his feet and hurled himself at his rival on the maple-branch. Round and round they would go, squeaking and chattering, but never ruffling a feather. Hour after hour, with brief intervals, and at times day after day, these two little hot but happy spirits played the comedy of this mimic war. It was not even a tempest in a teapot; it was tempest in a nutshell, but there was a vast deal of nature in it for all that. Both birds simply overflowed with the emotions proper to the season and the conditions.

The mate of the grape-post bird had a nest in a box farther down the hill, where the care of her young occupied her most of her time. She scolded as only wrens can scold when I went poking about her box, but my poking about the box of the male did not agitate the owner at all. I tried to explore the inside with my finger, but found it apparently

packed full of twigs. I had often seen the bird
enter it and disappear for some moments, but my
finger found no vacant space. Then one day I saw
the female enter it, much to the joy and loud ac-
claim of her mate. I finally saw her carry in fine
spears of dry grass. To clear up the mystery I
took off the top of the box, and found that there
was barely room enough between its top and the
twigs for a body the size of my finger to squeeze
in, and enter a small, deep pocket in one corner
which the cock had cunningly arranged. He had
made sure that no bird larger than a wren — no
usurping bluebird nor meddling English sparrow —
could gain entrance, and as for inquisitive wrens,
he could meet them at an advantage. Then I examined the lower box, where the young were, which
had an opening large enough for a high-hole, or a
great crested flycatcher, and found that the fore-
sighted little creatures had used the same tactics
here; they had built a barricade of twigs in front
of the nest, which was in one corner, and which
could be entered by the wrens only by a close
squeeze. Artful little people, I said, living joyous
and intensive lives, and as full of character and
spirit as an egg is full of meat.

This little bird loves to be near your house, but
give it a chance and it will come inside of it and nest
in the room you occupy. I knew of a pair that came
through a screen door left ajar, into a room on the

second floor of a famous inn in the valley of the Rondout, and built a nest on the sash behind a heavy green window-curtain — a real nest on one side of the door where the brood was raised, and a cock, or dummy, nest on the other side. It was not an inviting place for a nest, except that the room was occupied by a well-known woman artist and writer who seems to have extended a hearty welcome to the little feathered intruders. She cultivated them, and they seem to have cultivated her, sitting on the corner of her table when she was at work, and chattering and singing to her in the most pointed manner. The people in the house who knew of the situation were not slow in coming to the conclusion that the birds recognized in the artist a kindred spirit, and were drawn to her as they are not to other people. The case is at least a suggestive one.

I can relate but one somewhat analogous experience from my own life — remotely analogous, I may say, as I was not alone concerned in the case and the bird involved was not a wren. Some years ago, while on a visit to friends in one of the large cities of the western part of New York State, some members of a bird club and one or two officials of the city government drove me about through the various parks. We came to a park where there was a small aviary, a space thirty or forty feet square, enclosed by wire netting. In this cage were a number of our common birds, but the one that made a lasting impression upon me, and upon all who accompanied me, was a fox sparrow. No sooner had we paused before the big cage than a strange excitement seemed to seize this bird, and it began flying from one end of the enclosure to the other, clinging for a moment to the wires at each end, and singing in the most ecstatic manner, and by its enthusiasm kindling one or two other birds into song. I had heard the fox sparrow many times, but never before one that approached this one in power and brilliancy. It sang in a strain varied and copious beyond compare — a kind of musical frenzy. It was fairly startling. The man in charge said he had never heard it sing before, nor had any of my companions. I saw at once that the thought in all minds, which soon came out in words, was that the bird was singing to me; that it had recognized me as a bird-lover, and was intoxicated by the discovery. There were other bird-lovers in the company. There is, of course, some other explanation of the extraordinary performance, but what it is no one could suggest. There was nothing striking or unusual in the appearance of any of us, yet our presence seemed to act like fire to a fuse, and that one bird was the rocket that astonished and delighted us all. It darted about the enclosure as if its joy were uncontrollable, and sang in a spirit to match. I venture to say that none of those present will ever forget the incident. The more I thought about it afterward, the more it impressed me. I am not the least bit credulous about such things; I have never observed that the birds, or other wild creatures, behave in any way exceptionally toward me, or toward any one else. The legends in the old literature of the power of certain saintly persons, like St. Francis of Assisi, over the birds and animals, I look upon as legends merely. They are probably greatly exaggerated accounts of the power of gentleness and kindliness over the lower orders. The movements, the tones of the voice, the expression of the face, all play a part in the impression we make upon man or beast. I have always been successful in handling bees, because I am not afraid of bees, and go among them as if I had a right there. I am successful in making friends with dogs, because I show no suspicion or hesitancy toward them, and, as it were, extend to them the hand of fellowship. But the case of the fox sparrow is the single incident I can recall that might be interpreted, in the spirit of the old legends, as showing special sympathy and understanding between man and birds. The incident of the woman artist with the wrens nesting in her room, and their perching on her table and talking wren-talk to her, is of the same character. Such things may afford hints of some psychic condition, some community of mind between the human and the animal, as yet but little understood, but they are far from convincing.

A HAY-BARN IDYL

EVERY farm boy knows how much wild life ebbs and flows about a country hay-barn the whole year round. It is a point in the landscape where the wild and the domestic meet. The foxes prowl around it in winter, the squirrels visit it, mice and rats make their homes in it, and cut their roads through the hay. In summer swallows, phœbe-birds, and robins love to shelter their nests beneath its roof, bumblebees build their rude combs in the abandoned mice-nests, and yellow-jackets often hang their paper habitations from its timbers.

For several summers, as I have said in a former chapter, I have had my study in one of these empty or partly filled hay-barns on the farm where I was born, and the wild life about me that used to interest me as a boy now engages me as a student and observer of outdoor nature. While I am busy with my books and my writing, the birds are busy with their nest-building or brood-rearing. Now, in early July, a pair of barn swallows have a nest in the peak at one end, and a pair of phœbe-birds have a nest in the peak at the other end. The phœbes, remembering perhaps their ill luck last year, when their nest and eggs were buried by the hay-gatherers, have established themselves in a swallow's old nest far above any possibility of being engulfed by the rising tide of hay. They have evidently refurnished the nest, but its exterior is quite destitute of the moss with which they always face their structures. I see the row of heads of the young above the brim, as I see a row of heads of young swallows above the brim of their nest. The swallows evidently look upon the phœbes as intruders. Maybe the fact that the phœbes have appropriated a swallow's last year's nest rankles a little. At any rate, many times during the day the male swallow swoops spitefully down at the phœbes as they sit upon the beams hesitating in my presence to approach their nest with food in their beaks.

The swallow is not armed for battle; in both beak and claw he is about the weakest of the weak; only in speed and skill of wing is he almost unrivaled, and he flashes those long, slender, sabre-colored wings about the heads of his plain unwelcome neighbors in a way that keeps them on the alert, but never provokes them to retaliation. The phœbes incline this way and that to avoid the blows, but make no sound and raise no wing in defense. They seem to know what a big " bluff " the swallows are putting up, or else how unequal a wing contest with them would be.

The phœbes are much more sensitive to my presence than are the swallows; they will not betray the secret of their nest to me while I am watching them. Whereas the swallows sweep in boldly over my head through the wide-open doors, and, in a swift upward curve, touch at the nest and are out again like spirits, the phœbes enter slyly, through small openings in the weather-boards, and alight upon a beam and look the ground over before they approach the nest.

The other day in my walk I came upon two phœbes' nests under overhanging rocks, both with half-fledged young in them, and in neither case were the parent birds in evidence. They did not give their secret away by setting up the hue and cry that nesting birds usually set up on such occasions. I finally saw them, as silent as shadows, perched near by, with food in their beaks, which they finally swallowed as my stay was prolonged. And the nests, both on a level with my eye, were apparently filled only with a motionless mass of bluish mould. As I gently touched them, instead of four or five heads with open mouths springing up, the young only settled lower in the nest and disposed themselves in a headless, shapeless mass. The phœbe is evidently a very cautious bird, though none is more familiar about our porches and outbuildings.

What a contrast they present in habits and manners with the swallows! — the plebeian phœbe, plain of dress, homely of speech, with neither grace of form

Chewink

nor of movement, yet endeared to us by a hundred associations. The swallow has the grace of form and power of wing of the tireless sea-birds, and is almost as helpless and awkward on its feet as are some of the latter. The pair I am watching flash out and in the old barn like streaks of steel-blue lightning. I watch them hawking for insects over a broad meadow of timothy grass that slopes up to the woods that crown the hill. The mother bird is the more industrious; she makes at least three times as many trips in the course of an hour as does her mate; whether she returns with as loaded a beak or not, I have no means of knowing, but would wager that she does. Among nearly all species of birds the mother is the main bread-winner. I have recently had under observation a nest of young bluebirds in a cavity made by a downy woodpecker in a small birch-tree, a section of which I brought from the woods last fall and fastened up to one corner of my porch. The mother bird had entire care of the brood, bringing food every few minutes all day long. Not till the last day that the young were in the nest did the male appear, and then he took entire charge, and the mother either went off on a holiday, or else some untoward fate befell her.

I look up from my writing scores of times during the day to see the two swallows coursing low over the meadow of rippling daisies and timothy, tacking, darting, rising, falling, now turning abruptly, now sweeping in wide circles, and, having secured the invisible morsel, coming down grade into the barn with the speed of arrows. A row of expectant heads, four or five of them, arranged along the wide opening of the nest await them. It is touch and go, no tarrying; the gnat or the fly is deposited in an open mouth as swiftly as it is caught. The beaks of all the young open as the swift wings of the parent bird are heard, and a subdued chippering and squeaking follows. That there is any method in the feeding, or that they are fed in regular order, I cannot believe. Which of the young will get the next morsel is probably a matter of chance, but doubtless the result averages up very evenly in the course of an hour or two.

The wing-power expended by the parent birds in this incessant and rapid flight must be very great, and one would think that all the insects captured would be required to keep it up. How fine and slight their prey seems to be! I may follow their course through the meadow with my head about as high above the grass as is their flight, and not see anything but an occasional butterfly or two — a game the swallows are not looking for. They hunt out something invisible to my eyes, something almost as intangible as the drifting flower pollen. Probably the finer it is, the more potent it is; a meal of gnats may be highly concentrated food. Now and then they probably capture a house-fly or other large insect. To know how full the summer air is of fine, gauzy insects, look toward the sun of an afternoon where you have the shadow of a wood for a background. The sunlight falling on the wings of the tiny creatures seems greatly to magnify them, and one sees where the speeding swallows reap much of their harvest.

The phœbe, and all the true flycatchers, hunt in a much less haphazard way; like the hawks, they see their prey before they make their swoop; they are true sportsmen and their aim is sure. Perched here and there, they wait for their game to appear. But the swallows hurl themselves through the air with tremendous speed and capture what chances to cross their paths — a feat quite impossible to the regular flycatcher.

On calm days they hawk high; on windy days their prey flies near the earth and they hunt low. How random and wayward their course is, but what freedom and power of wing it discloses! A poet has called them skaters in the field of air, but what skater can perform such gyrations or attain such speed? Occasionally on windy days they seem to dip and turn, or check themselves, as if they saw an individual insect and paused to seize it. But for the most part they seem to strain the air through their beaks and seize what it leaves them.

As the days pass, the young swallows begin to grow restless. I see them stretching their wings, with their bodies half out of the nest. A day or two later I hear a fluttering sound over my head and look up to see one of them clinging to the outside of the nest and exercising his wings vigorously; for a few seconds he clings there and makes his wings hum; the flying impulse is working on him, and soon it will launch him forth upon the air. Two or three times a day I see this feat repeated. The young are doubtless all taking turns in trying their wings to see if they are as recommended. Then the parents come in, evidently with empty beaks, and take turns in hovering in front of the nest and saying, "Wit, wit," approvingly and encouragingly, and then flying about the empty barn or making a dash at phœbe as she sits with flipping tail on a beam. Presently they resume their feeding. The next day there is more wing exercise by the young, and more hovering and chirping about the nest by the parents. Sometimes the latter sit quietly upon a beam, and then the male flies up and clings for a moment to the side of the nest, and squeaks softly and lovingly. I think the great event, the first flight of the young, is near at hand. I go to dinner and when I return and am about to enter the barn, the mother swallow sweeps down toward me and calls "Sleet, sleet," which I take to be her way of saying "Scat, scat," and I know something has happened. Looking up to the roof, I see one of the young perched upon it a few inches from the lower edge. He looks scared and ill at ease. I cast a pebble above him and away he goes into the free air, his parents wheeling about him, and leading him on in an evident state of excitement. How well he used his wings on that first flight, swooping and soaring with but little appearance of awkwardness or hesitation. After a few moments he comes back to the barn roof and alights on the other side beyond my sight. During the afternoon the other three venture out at intervals and fly about the interior of the barn for some time before venturing outside, their parents flying with them and cheering encouragingly.

When once launched on the wing, the next great problem with them seemed to be how to alight. It was evidently a trying problem. They would make feints at stopping upon this beam or upon that, but could not quite manage it till, in an awkward manner, they would flop down somewhere. In a good many things we ourselves find it more difficult to stop than to start. In the course of the afternoon they all went forth into the air with their parents, and, I think, never returned to the interior of the barn. At five o'clock I saw them perched upon the tops of dry mullein-stalks in the pasture. As I approached them, they took flight and coursed through the air high and low, over the tree-tops and above the valley, with wonderful ease and freedom. After a while they returned to the mullein-stalks and again betrayed their inexperience by their awkwardness in alighting. It would be interesting to know how long they were on the wing before they began capturing their own food. I saw the parent birds feeding them in the air a few days after the exodus from the nest. In August they will be perching upon telegraph-wires and upon the ridgepoles of hay-barns, with the instinct of migration working in their little bodies.

The exodus of the young phœbes from the nest was much less noticeable. I saw no preliminary stretching or flapping of wings, and no parental solicitude. Flying is not the business of the phœbe, as it is with the swallow, and its life is much more humdrum. The young came out at intervals one afternoon, and they lingered about the barn, going out and in for several days, the family keeping well together. Later I shall see them about the orchards and fences, bobbing their tails and being fed by their parents.

A mow of last year's hay in the big bay of the barn holds its pretty secret also. Two years ago a junco or snowbird built her nest in its side, and this year she, or another, is back again, a month earlier. It amuses me to see her come in with her beak full of dry grass to build a nest in a mow of dry grass. Her forebears have always built their nests in the sides of weedy or mossgrown banks in secluded fields and woodsides, and have used such material as they could find in these places. She is under the spell of these inherited habits — in all but in the selection of the locality of her nest. In this she makes a new departure, and in so doing shows how adaptive many of the wild creatures are. The bird has probably failed in her attempts to bring out a brood in the old places. I think three out of four of all such attempts on the part of ground builders do fail. Within a few days two sparrows' nests in a small space in the pasture below me have been "harried," as the Scotch say. If they escape the sharp-eyed crows by day, the skunks and the foxes, or other night prowlers, are pretty sure to smell them out by night. The family of crows, two old ones and four young ones, that I see every day foraging about the fields, probably plunder nine out of ten of all the nests in the field. At any rate, my junco has decided on trying the shelter of the old barn. Here she is in danger from rats and cats and red squirrels, but at this season she stands a fair chance of escape. When she comes in with a wisp of the outdoor rubbish in her beak, I should say she showed some nervousness were it not for the fact that juncoes always seem to be nervous. She flits about with her eye upon me, and after a few feints flies up to her place on the side of the mow and disappears for a moment under the drooping locks of hay. Her nest is completed in two or three forenoons — a very simple and rude affair compared with the nest in May or June under a mossy bank by the woodside. Then she is not in evidence for two or three days, when, one morning, I discover that the nest holds two eggs. Two days later it holds four, and the next day incubation has evidently begun. As she sits in the shadow of her little cavity in the mow, only her light-colored beak shows me when she is on her nest. A heavy rope is stretched low across the barn floor, and it is a pretty sight to see her approach the hay-mow along this rope, hopping nervously along, showing the white quills in her tail, and wiping her beak over and over on the rope as she progresses. I think the beak-wiping, now on this side, now on that, is just another expression of her nervousness, or else of preoccupation, for surely her beak is clean. She gives no heed either to the swallows or to the phœbes, nor they to her. Well, she is fairly launched on her little voyage of maternity, and I shall do all I can to see that her venture is successful.

A week later, alas! it turned out to be the old story of the best-laid schemes of mice and men. Some serious mishap befell my little neighbor. One day she was missing from her nest from morning till night. The following morning her eggs were stone cold, and the male bird was flitting about the barn and running along the beams as I entered, no doubt in an anxious state of mind about his mate. I could give him no clue to her whereabouts, and her fate is a mystery — whether captured, by a hawk or a cat, while out in quest of food, I shall never know.

The same day ill fortune overtook a queen bumble-bee who had a nest somewhere about the barn. She appeared abruptly upon the ground in front of my door in a great state of excitement. She seemed suddenly to have discovered that she could not fly, and she was making vain attempts to do so, in a state of painful agitation. She buzzed and rushed about amid the dry grass and loose straws like one beside herself. I went to her to give her a lift; she rushed up the twig I proffered, then up my hand, shaking with excitement. From this coign of vantage she tried to launch herself into the air, but fell ingloriously to the ground. I saw that her right wing was badly mutilated; not more than half of it remained, and flying was out of the question. But the poor queen would not have it so; she could not be convinced that she could not fly. The oftener she failed in her attempts, the more desperate she became. She always had flown, and now suddenly her wings failed her. She would climb up the taller spears of grass and make the attempt, and upon stems and sticks. She could not accept her cruel fate. She finally rushed into the stonework and I saw her no more.

I am not certain that the queen bumblebee makes a nuptial flight like the queen of the hive bees, but probably she does, and this one may have left her near-by colony for this purpose, only to flounder ingloriously among the weeds. Probably some anarchist insect had frayed and clipped her wing in her nest, having no more respect for royalty than for her humble subjects. There is no sphere of life so lowly that such tragedies and failures do not come to it.

A SHARP LOOKOUT

ONE has only to sit down in the woods or the fields, or by the shore of the river or the lake, and nearly everything of interest will come round to him, — the birds, the animals, the insects; and presently, after his eye has got accustomed to the place, and to the light and shade, he will probably see some plant or flower that he has sought in vain, and that is a pleasant surprise to him. So, on a large scale, the student and lover of nature has this advantage over people who gad up and down the world, seeking some novelty or excitement; he has only to stay at home and see the procession pass. The great globe swings around to him like a revolving showcase; the change of the seasons is like the passage of strange and new countries; the zones of the earth, with all their beauties and marvels, pass one's door, and linger long in the passing. What a voyage is this we make without leaving for a night our own fireside! St. Pierre well says that a sense of the power and mystery of nature shall spring up as fully in one's heart after he has made the circuit of his own field as after returning from a voyage round the world. I sit here amid the junipers of the Hudson, with purpose every year to go to Florida, or to the West Indies, or to the Pacific coast, yet the seasons pass and I am still loitering, with a half-defined suspicion, perhaps, that, if I remain quiet and keep a sharp lookout, these countries will come to me. I may stick it out yet, and not miss much after all. The great trouble is for Mohammed to know when the mountain really comes to him. Sometimes a rabbit or a jay or a little warbler brings the woods to my door. A loon on the river, and the Canada lakes are here; the sea-gulls and the fish hawk bring the sea; the call of the wild gander at night, what does it suggest? and the eagle flapping by, or floating along on a raft of ice, does not he bring the mountain? One spring morning five swans flew above my barn in single file, going northward, — an express train bound for Labrador. It was a more exhilarating sight than if I had seen them in their native haunts. They made a breeze in my mind, like a noble passage in a poem. How gently their great wings flapped; how easy to fly when spring gives the impulse! On another occasion I saw a line of fowls, probably swans, going northward, at such a height that they appeared like a faint, waving black line against the sky. They must have been at an altitude of two or three miles.

I was looking intently at the clouds to see which way they moved, when the birds came into my field of vision. I should never have seen them had they not crossed the precise spot upon which my eye was fixed. As it was near sundown, they were probably launched for an all-night pull. They were going with great speed, and as they swayed a little this way and that, they suggested a slender, all but invisible, aerial serpent cleaving the ether. What a highway was pointed out up there! — an easy grade from the Gulf to Hudson's Bay.

Then the typical spring and summer and autumn days, of all shades and complexions, — one cannot afford to miss any of them; and when looked out upon from one's own spot of earth, how much more beautiful and significant they are! Nature comes home to one most when he is at home; the stranger and traveler finds her a stranger and traveler also. One's own landscape comes in time to be a sort of outlying part of himself; he has sowed himself broadcast upon it, and it reflects his own moods and feelings; he is sensitive to the verge of the horizon : cut those trees, and he bleeds ; mar those hills, and he suffers. How has the farmer planted himself in his fields; builded himself into his stone walls, and evoked the sympathy of the hills by his struggle! This home feeling, this domestication of nature, is important to the observer. This is the bird-lime with which he catches the bird; this is

Blue Jay

the private door that admits him behind the scenes. This is one source of Gilbert White's charm, and of the charm of Thoreau's " Walden."

The birds that come about one's door in winter, or that build in his trees in summer, what a peculiar interest they have! What crop have I sowed in Florida or in California, that I should go there to reap? I should be only a visitor, or formal caller upon nature, and the family would all wear masks. No; the place to observe nature is where you are; the walk to take to-day is the walk you took yesterday. You will not find just the same things: both the observed and the observer have changed; the ship is on another tack in both cases.

I shall probably never see another just such day as yesterday was, because one can never exactly repeat his observation, — cannot turn the leaf of the book of life backward, — and because each day has characteristics of its own. This was a typical March day, clear, dry, hard, and windy, the river rumpled and crumpled, the sky intense, distant objects strangely near; a day full of strong light, unusual; an extraordinary lightness and clearness all around the horizon, as if there were a diurnal aurora streaming up and burning through the sunlight; smoke from the first spring fires rising up in various directions; a day that winnowed the air, and left no film in the sky. At night, how the big March bellows did work! Venus was like a great lamp in the sky. The stars all seemed brighter than usual, as if the wind blew them up like burning coals. Venus actually seemed to flare in the wind.

Each day foretells the next, if one could read the signs; to-day is the progenitor of to-morrow. When the atmosphere is telescopic, and distant objects stand out unusually clear and sharp, a storm is near. We are on the crest of the wave, and the depression follows quickly. It often happens that clouds are not so indicative of a storm as the total absence of clouds. In this state of the atmosphere the stars are unusually numerous and bright at night, which is also a bad omen.

I find this observation confirmed by Humboldt. " It appears," he says, " that the transparency of the air is prodigiously increased when a certain quantity of water is uniformly diffused through it." Again, he says that the mountaineers of the Alps " predict a change of weather when, the air being calm, the Alps covered with perpetual snow seem on a sudden to be nearer the observer, and their outlines are marked with great distinctness on the azure sky." He further observes that the same condition of the atmosphere renders distant sounds more audible.

There is one redness in the east in the morning that means storm, another that means wind. The former is broad, deep, and angry; the clouds look like a huge bed of burning coals just raked open;

the latter is softer, more vapory, and more widely extended. Just at the point where the sun is going to rise, and some minutes in advance of his coming, there sometimes rises straight upward a rosy column; it is like a shaft of deeply dyed vapor, blending with and yet partly separated from the clouds, and the base of which presently comes to glow like the sun itself. The day that follows is pretty certain to be very windy. At other times the under sides of the eastern clouds are all turned to pink or rose-colored wool; the transformation extends until nearly the whole sky flushes, even the west glowing slightly; the sign is always to be interpreted as meaning fair weather.

The approach of great storms is seldom heralded by any striking or unusual phenomenon. The real weather gods are free from brag and bluster; but the sham gods fill the sky with portentous signs and omens. I recall one 5th of March as a day that would have filled the ancient observers with dreadful forebodings. At ten o'clock the sun was attended by four extraordinary sun-dogs. A large bright halo encompassed him, on the top of which the segment of a larger circle rested, forming a sort of heavy brilliant crown. At the bottom of the circle, and depending from it, was a mass of soft, glowing, iridescent vapor. On either side, like fragments of the larger circle, were two brilliant arcs. Altogether, it was the most portentous storm-breeding sun I ever beheld. In a dark hemlock wood in a valley, the owls were hooting ominously, and the crows dismally cawing. Before night the storm set in, a little sleet and rain of a few hours' duration, insignificant enough compared with the signs and wonders that preceded it.

To what extent the birds or animals can foretell the weather is uncertain. When the swallows are seen hawking very high, it is a good indication; the insects upon which they feed venture up there only in the most auspicious weather. Yet bees will continue to leave the hive when a storm is imminent. I am told that one of the most reliable weather signs they have down in Texas is afforded by the ants. The ants bring their eggs up out of their underground retreats and expose them to the warmth of the sun to be hatched. When they are seen carrying them in again in great haste, though there be not a cloud in the sky, your walk or your drive must be postponed: a storm is at hand. There is a passage in Virgil that is doubtless intended to embody a similar observation, though none of his translators seem to have hit its meaning accurately: —

" Sæpius et tectis penetralibus extulit ova
    Angustum formica terens iter; "

" Often also has the pismire making a narrow road brought forth her eggs out of the hidden recesses," is the literal translation of old John Martyn.

" Also the ant, incessantly traveling
   The same straight way with the eggs of her hidden
      store,''

is one of the latest metrical translations. Dryden
has it: —

" The careful ant her secret cell forsakes
   And drags her eggs along the narrow tracks,''

which comes nearer to the fact. When a storm is
coming, Virgil also makes his swallows skim low
about the lake, which agrees with the observation
above.

The critical moments of the day as regards the
weather are at sunrise and sunset. A clear sunset
is always a good sign; an obscured sun, just at the
moment of going down after a bright day, bodes
storm. There is much truth, too, in the saying
that if it rain before seven, it will clear before
eleven. Nine times in ten it will turn out thus.
The best time for it to begin to rain or snow, if it
wants to hold out, is about mid-forenoon. The
great storms usually begin at this time. On all
occasions the weather is very sure to declare itself
before eleven o'clock. If you are going on a picnic, or are going to start on a journey, and the
morning is unsettled, wait till ten and one half
o'clock, and you will know what the remainder
of the day will be. Midday clouds and afternoon
clouds, except in the season of thunderstorms, are

usually harmless idlers and vagabonds. But more to be relied on than any obvious sign is that subtle perception of the condition of the weather which a man has who spends much of his time in the open air. He can hardly tell how he knows it is going to rain; he hits the fact as an Indian does the mark with his arrow, without calculating and by a kind of sure instinct. As you read a man's purpose in his face, so you learn to read the purpose of the weather in the face of the day.

In observing the weather, however, as in the diagnosis of disease, the diathesis is all-important. All signs fail in a drought, because the predisposition, the diathesis, is so strongly toward fair weather; and the opposite signs fail during a wet spell, because nature is caught in the other rut.

Observe the lilies of the field. Sir John Lubbock says the dandelion lowers itself after flowering, and lies close to the ground while it is maturing its seed, and then rises up. It is true that the dandelion lowers itself after flowering, retires from society, as it were, and meditates in seclusion; but after it lifts itself up again, the stalk begins anew to grow, it lengthens daily, keeping just above the grass till the fruit is ripened, and the little globe of silvery down is carried many inches higher than was the ring of golden flowers. And the reason is obvious. The plant depends upon the wind to scatter its seeds; every one of these little vessels spreads a sail to the breeze, and it is necessary that they be launched above the grass and weeds, amid which they would be caught and held did the stalk not continue to grow and outstrip the rival vegetation. It is a curious instance of foresight in a weed.

I wish I could read as clearly this puzzle of the button-balls (American plane-tree). Why has Nature taken such particular pains to keep these balls hanging to the parent tree intact till spring? What secret of hers has she buttoned in so securely? for these buttons will not come off. The wind cannot twist them off, nor warm nor wet hasten or retard them. The stem, or peduncle, by which the ball is held in the fall and winter, breaks up into a dozen or more threads or strands, that are stronger than those of hemp. When twisted tightly they make a little cord that I find impossible to break with my hands. Had they been longer, the Indian would surely have used them to make his bowstrings and all the other strings he required. One could hang himself with a small cord of them. (In South America, Humboldt saw excellent cordage made by the Indians from the petioles of the Chiquichiqui palm.) Nature has determined that these buttons should stay on. In order that the seeds of this tree may germinate, it is probably necessary that they be kept dry during the winter, and reach the ground after the season of warmth and moisture is fully established. In May, just as the leaves and the new balls are emerging, at the touch of a warm, moist south wind, these spherical packages suddenly go to pieces — explode, in fact, like tiny bombshells that were fused to carry to this point — and scatter their seeds to the four winds. They yield at the same time a fine pollen-like dust that one would suspect played some part in fertilizing the new balls, did not botany teach him otherwise. At any rate, it is the only deciduous tree I know of that does not let go the old seed till the new is well on the way. It is plain why the sugar-berry-tree or lotus holds its drupes all winter: it is in order that the birds may come and sow the seed. The berries are like small gravel-stones with a sugar coating, and a bird will not eat them till he is pretty hard pressed, but in late fall and winter the robins, cedar-birds, and bluebirds devour them readily, and of course lend their wings to scatter the seed far and wide. The same is true of juniper-berries, and the fruit of the bitter-sweet.

In certain other cases where the fruit tends to hang on during the winter, as with the bladder-nut and the honey-locust, it is probably because the frost and the perpetual moisture of the ground would rot or kill the germ. To beechnuts, chestnuts, and acorns the moisture of the ground and the covering of leaves seem congenial, though too much warmth and moisture often cause the acorns

213

to germinate prematurely. I have found the ground under the oaks in December covered with nuts, all anchored to the earth by purple sprouts. But the winter which follows such untimely growths generally proves fatal to them.

One must always cross-question nature if he would get at the truth, and he will not get at it then unless he frames his questions with great skill. Most persons are unreliable observers because they put only leading questions, or vague questions.

Perhaps there is nothing in the operations of nature to which we can properly apply the term intelligence, yet there are many things that at first sight look like it. Place a tree or plant in an unusual position and it will prove itself equal to the occasion, and behave in an unusual manner; it will show original resources; it will seem to try intelligently to master the difficulties. Up by Furlow Lake, where I was camping out, a young hemlock had become established upon the end of a large and partly decayed log that reached many feet out into the lake. The young tree was eight or nine feet high; it had sent its roots down into the log and clasped it around on the outside, and had apparently discovered that there was water instead of soil immediately beneath it, and that its sustenance must be sought elsewhere and that quickly. Accordingly it had started one large root, by far the largest of all, for the shore along the top of the log. This root, when I saw the tree, was six or seven feet long, and had bridged more than half the distance that separated the tree from the land.

Was this a kind of intelligence ? If the shore had lain in the other direction, no doubt at all but the root would have started for the other side. I know a yellow pine that stands on the side of a steep hill. To make its position more secure, it has thrown out a large root at right angles with its stem directly into the bank above it, which acts as a stay or guy-rope. It was positively the best thing the tree could do. The earth has washed away so that the root where it leaves the tree is two feet above the surface of the soil.

Yet both these cases are easily explained, and without attributing any power of choice, or act of intelligent selection, to the trees. In the case of the little hemlock upon the partly submerged log, roots were probably thrown out equally in all directions ; on all sides but one they reached the water and stopped growing; the water checked them; but on the land side, the root on the top of the log, not meeting with any obstacle of the kind, kept on growing, and thus pushing its way toward the shore. It was a case of survival, not of the fittest, but of that which the situation favored, — the fittest with reference to position.

So with the pine-tree on the side of the hill. It probably started its roots in all directions, but only the one on the upper side survived and matured. Those on the lower side finally perished, and others lower down took their places. Thus the whole life upon the globe, as we see it, is the result of this blind groping and putting forth of Nature in every direction, with failure of some of her ventures and the success of others, the circumstances, the environments, supplying the checks and supplying the stimulus, the seed falling upon the barren places just the same as upon the fertile. No discrimination on the part of Nature that we can express in the terms of our own consciousness, but ceaseless experiments in every possible direction. The only thing inexplicable is the inherent impulse to experiment, the original push, the principle of Life.

The good observer of nature holds his eye long and firmly to the point, as one does when looking at a puzzle picture, and will not be baffled. The cat catches the mouse, not merely because she watches for him, but because she is armed to catch him and is quick. So the observer finally gets the fact, not only because he has patience, but because his eye is sharp and his inference swift. Many a shrewd old farmer looks upon the milky way as a kind of weathercock, and will tell you that the way it points at night indicates the direction of the wind the following day. So, also, every new moon is either a dry moon or a wet moon, dry if a powder-horn would hang upon the lower limb, wet if it would not; forgetting the fact that, as a rule, when it is dry in one part of the continent it is wet in some other part, and *vice versa*. When he kills his hogs in the fall, if the pork be very hard and solid, he predicts a severe winter; if soft and loose, the opposite; again overlooking the fact that the kind of food and the temperature of the fall make the pork hard or make it soft. So with a hundred other signs, all the result of hasty and incomplete observations.

One season, the last day of December was very warm. The bees were out of the hive, and there was no frost in the air or in the ground. I was walking in the woods, when as I paused in the shade of a hemlock-tree I heard a sound proceed from beneath the wet leaves on the ground but a few feet from me that suggested a frog. Following it cautiously up, I at last determined upon the exact spot whence the sound issued; lifting up the thick layer of leaves, there sat a frog — the wood frog, one of the first to appear in the marshes in spring, and which I have elsewhere called the " clucking frog " — in a little excavation in the surface of the leaf mould. As it sat there, the top of its back was level with the surface of the ground. This, then, was its hibernaculum; here it was prepared to pass the winter, with only a coverlid of wet matted leaves between it and zero weather. Forthwith I set up as a prophet of warm weather, and among other things

predicted a failure of the ice crop on the river;
which, indeed, others, who had not heard frogs
croak on the 31st of December, had also begun to
predict. Surely, I thought, this frog knows what
it is about; here is the wisdom of nature; it would
have gone deeper into the ground than that if a severe winter was approaching; so I was not anxious
about my coal-bin, nor disturbed by longings for
Florida. But what a winter followed, the winter
of 1885, when the Hudson became coated with ice
nearly two feet thick, and when March was as cold
as January! I thought of my frog under the hemlock and wondered how it was faring. So one day
the latter part of March, when the snow was gone,
and there was a feeling of spring in the air, I turned
aside in my walk to investigate it. The matted
leaves were still frozen hard, but I succeeded in lifting them up and exposing the frog. There it sat
as fresh and unscathed as in the fall. The ground
beneath and all about it was still frozen like a
rock, but apparently it had some means of its own of
resisting the frost. It winked and bowed its head
when I touched it, but did not seem inclined to leave
its retreat. Some days later, after the frost was
nearly all out of the ground, I passed that way, and
found my frog had come out of its seclusion and
was resting amid the dry leaves. There was not
much jump in it yet, but its color was growing
lighter. A few more warm days, and its fellows, and

doubtless itself too, were croaking and gamboling in the marshes.

This incident convinced me of two things; namely, that frogs know no more about the coming weather than we do, and that they do not retreat as deep into the ground to pass the winter as has been supposed. I used to think the muskrats could foretell an early and a severe winter, and have so written. But I am now convinced they cannot; they know as little about it as I do. Sometimes on an early and severe frost they seem to get alarmed and go to building their houses, but usually they seem to build early or late, high or low, just as the whim takes them.

In most of the operations of nature there is at least one unknown quantity; to find the exact value of this unknown factor is not so easy. The wool of the sheep, the fur of the animals, the feathers of the fowls, the husks of the maize, why are they thicker some seasons than others; what is the value of the unknown quantity here? Does it indicate a severe winter approaching? Only observations extending over a series of years could determine the point. How much patient observation it takes to settle many of the facts in the lives of the birds, animals, and insects! Gilbert White was all his life trying to determine whether or not swallows passed the winter in a torpid state in the mud at the bottom of ponds and marshes; and he died ignorant of the truth that they do not. Do honey-bees injure the grape and other fruits by puncturing the skin for the juice? The most patient watching by many skilled eyes all over the country has not yet settled the point. For my own part, I am convinced that they do not. The honey-bee is not the rough-and-ready freebooter that the wasp and the bumblebee are; she has somewhat of feminine timidity, and leaves the first rude assaults to them. I knew the honey-bee was very fond of the locust blossoms, and that the trees hummed like a hive in the height of their flowering, but I did not know that the bumblebee was ever the sapper and miner that went ahead in this enterprise, till one day I placed myself amid the foliage of a locust and saw him savagely bite through the shank of the flower and extract the nectar, followed by a honey-bee that in every instance searched for this opening, and probed long and carefully for the leavings of her burly purveyor. The bumblebee rifles the dicentra and the columbine of their treasures in the same manner, namely, by slitting their pockets from the outside, and the honey-bee gleans after him, taking the small change he leaves. In the case of the locust, however, she usually obtains the honey without the aid of the larger bee.

Speaking of the honey-bee reminds me that the subtle and sleight-of-hand manner in which she fills her baskets with pollen and propolis is character-

istic of much of Nature's doings. See the bee
going from flower to flower with the golden pellets
on her thighs, slowly and mysteriously increasing
in size. If the miller were to take the toll of the
grist he grinds by gathering the particles of flour
from his coat and hat, as he moved rapidly about,
or catching them in his pockets, he would be doing
pretty nearly what the bee does. The little miller
dusts herself with the pollen of the flower, and
then, while on the wing, brushes it off with the
fine brush on certain of her feet, and by some jug-
glery or other catches it in her pollen basket. One
needs to look long and intently to see through the
trick. Pliny says they fill their baskets with their
fore feet, and that they fill their fore feet with
their trunks, but it is a much more subtle operation
than this. I have seen the bees come to a meal
barrel in early spring, and to a pile of hardwood
sawdust before there was yet anything in nature for
them to work upon, and, having dusted their coats
with the finer particles of the meal or the sawdust,
hover on the wing above the mass till the little
legerdemain feat was performed. Nature fills her
baskets by the same sleight-of-hand, and the observer must be on the alert who would possess her
secret. If the ancients had looked a little closer
and sharper, would they ever have believed in
spontaneous generation in the superficial way in
which they did ; that maggots, for instance, were gen-

erated spontaneously in putrid flesh? Could they not see the spawn of the blow-flies? Or, if Virgil had been a real observer of the bees, would he ever have credited, as he certainly appears to do, the fable of bees originating from the carcass of a steer? or that on windy days they carried little stones for ballast? or that two hostile swarms fought each other in the air? Indeed, the ignorance, or the false science, of the ancient observers, with regard to the whole subject of bees, is most remarkable; not false science merely with regard to their more hidden operations, but with regard to that which is open and patent to all who have eyes in their heads, and have ever had to do with them. And Pliny names authors who had devoted their whole lives to the study of the subject.

But the ancients, like women and children, were not accurate observers. Just at the critical moment their eyes were unsteady, or their fancy, or their credulity, or their impatience, got the better of them, so that their science was half fact and half fable. Thus, for instance, because the young cuckoo at times appeared to take the head of its small foster mother quite into its mouth while receiving its food, they believed that it finally devoured her. Pliny, who embodied the science of his times in his natural history, says of the wasp that it carries spiders to its nest, and then sits upon them until it hatches its young from them. A little careful observation would have shown him that this was only a half truth; that the whole truth was, that the spiders were entombed with the egg of the wasp to serve as food for the young when the egg had hatched.

What curious questions Plutarch discusses, as, for instance, "What is the reason that a bucket of water drawn out of a well, if it stands all night in the air that is in the well, is more cold in the morning than the rest of the water?" He could probably have given many reasons why "a watched pot never boils." The ancients, the same author says, held that the bodies of those killed by lightning never putrefy; that the sight of a ram quiets an enraged elephant; that a viper will lie stock-still if touched by a beechen leaf; that a wild bull grows tame if bound with the twigs of a fig-tree; that a hen purifies herself with straw after she has laid an egg; that the deer buries his cast-off horns; and that a goat stops the whole herd by holding a branch of the sea-holly in his mouth. They sought to account for such things without stopping to ask, Are they true? Nature was too novel, or else too fearful, to them to be deliberately pursued and hunted down. Their youthful joy in her, or their dread and awe in her presence, may be better than our scientific satisfaction, or cool wonder, or our vague, mysterious sense of "something far more deeply interfused;" yet we cannot change with them if we would, and I, for one, would not if I could. Science does not mar nature. The railroad, Thoreau found, after all, to be about the wildest road he knew of, and the telegraph wires the best æolian harp out of doors. Study of nature deepens the mystery and the charm because it removes the horizon farther off. We cease to fear, perhaps, but how can one cease to marvel and to love?

The fields and woods and waters about one are a book from which he may draw exhaustless entertainment, if he will. One must not only learn the writing, he must translate the language, the signs, and the hieroglyphics. It is a very quaint and elliptical writing, and much must be supplied by the wit of the translator. At any rate, the lesson is to be well conned. Gilbert White said that that locality would be found the richest in zoölogical or botanical specimens which was most thoroughly examined. For more than forty years he studied the ornithology of his district without exhausting the subject. I thought I knew my own tramping-ground pretty well, but one April day, when I looked a little closer than usual into a small semi-stagnant lakelet where I had peered a hundred times before, I suddenly discovered scores of little creatures that were as new to me as so many nymphs would have been. They were partly fish-shaped, from an inch to an inch and a half long, semi-transparent, with a dark brownish line visible the entire length of them (apparently the thread upon which the life of the animal hung, and by which its all but impalpable frame was held together), and suspending themselves in the water, or impelling themselves swiftly forward by means of a double row of fine, waving, hair-like appendages, that arose from what appeared to be the back, — a kind of undulating, pappus-like wings. What was it? I did not know. None of my friends or scientific acquaintances knew. I wrote to a learned man, an authority upon fish, describing the creature as well as I could. He replied that it was only a familiar species of phyllopodous crustacean, known as *Eubranchipus vernalis*.

I remember that our guide in the Maine woods, seeing I had names of my own for some of the plants, would often ask me the name of this and that flower for which he had no word; and that when I could recall the full Latin term, it seemed overwhelmingly convincing and satisfying to him. It was evidently a relief to know that these obscure plants of his native heath had been found worthy of a learned name, and that the Maine woods were not so uncivil and outlandish as they might at first seem: it was a comfort to him to know that he did not live beyond the reach of botany. In like manner I found satisfaction in knowing that my novel fish had been recognized and worthily named; the title conferred a new dignity at once; but when the

learned man added that it was familiarly called the
" fairy shrimp," I felt a deeper pleasure. Fairy-
like it certainly was, in its aerial, unsubstantial
look, and in its delicate, down-like means of loco-
motion; but the large head, with its curious folds,
and its eyes standing out in relief, as if on the
heads of two pins, was gnome-like. Probably the
fairy wore a mask, and wanted to appear terrible
to human eyes. Then the creatures had sprung out
of the earth as by magic. I found some in a furrow in a plowed field that had encroached upon a
swamp. In the fall the plow had been there, and
had turned up only the moist earth ; now a little
water was standing there, from which the April
sunbeams had invoked these airy, fairy creatures.
They belong to the crustaceans, but apparently no
creature has so thin or impalpable a crust; you can
almost see through them ; certainly you can see
what they have had for dinner, if they have eaten
substantial food.

All we know about the private and essential
natural history of the bees, the birds, the fishes,
the animals, the plants, is the result of close, patient, quick-witted observation. Yet Nature will
often elude one for all his pains and alertness.
Thoreau, as revealed in his journal, was for years
trying to settle in his own mind what was the first
thing that stirred in spring, after the severe New
England winter, — in what was the first sign or

pulse of returning life manifest; and he never seems to have been quite sure. He could not get his salt on the tail of this bird. He dug into the swamps, he peered into the water, he felt with benumbed hands for the radical leaves of the plants under the snow; he inspected the buds on the willows, the catkins on the alders; he went out before daylight of a March morning and remained out after dark; he watched the lichens and mosses on the rocks; he listened for the birds; he was on the alert for the first frog (" Can you be absolutely sure," he says, " that you have heard the first frog that croaked in the township? "); he stuck a pin here and he stuck a pin there, and there, and still he could not satisfy himself. Nor can any one. Life appears to start in several things simultaneously. Of a warm thawy day in February the snow is suddenly covered with myriads of snow fleas looking like black, new powder just spilled there. Or you may see a winged insect in the air. On the selfsame day the grass in the spring run and the catkins on the alders will have started a little; and if you look sharply, while passing along some sheltered nook or grassy slope where the sunshine lies warm on the bare ground, you will probably see a grasshopper or two. The grass hatches out under the snow, and why should not the grasshopper? At any rate, a few such hardy specimens may be found in the latter part of our milder winters wherever the sun has uncovered a sheltered bit of grass for a few days, even after a night of ten or twelve degrees of frost. Take them in the shade, and let them freeze stiff as pokers, and when thawed out again they will hop briskly. And yet, if a poet were to put grasshoppers in his winter poem, we should require pretty full specifications of him, or else fur to clothe them with. Nature will not be cornered, yet she does many things in a corner and surreptitiously. She is all things to all men; she has whole truths, half truths, and quarter truths, if not still smaller fractions. The careful observer finds this out sooner or later. Old fox-hunters will tell you, on the evidence of their own eyes, that there is a black fox and a silver-gray fox, two species, but there are not ; the black fox is black when coming toward you or running from you, and silver gray at point-blank view, when the eye penetrates the fur; each separate hair is gray the first half and black the last. This is a sample of Nature's half truths.

Which are our sweet-scented wild flowers ? Put your nose to every flower you pluck, and you will be surprised how your list will swell the more you smell. I plucked some wild blue violets one day, the *ovata* variety of the *sagittata*, that had a faint perfume of sweet clover, but I never could find another that had any odor. A pupil disputed with his teacher about the hepatica, claiming in opposition that it was sweet-scented. Some hepaticas are sweet-scented and some are not, and the perfume is stronger some seasons than others. After the unusually severe winter of 1880–81, the variety of hepatica called the sharp-lobed was markedly sweet in nearly every one of the hundreds of specimens I examined. A handful of them exhaled a most delicious perfume. The white ones that season were largely in the ascendant; and probably the white specimens of both varieties, one season with another, will oftenest prove sweet-scented. Darwin says a considerably larger proportion of white flowers are sweet-scented than of any other color. The only sweet violets I can depend upon are white, *Viola blanda* and *Viola Canadensis*, and white largely predominates among our other odorous wild flowers. All the fruit trees have white or pinkish blossoms. I recall no native blue flower of New York or New England that is fragrant except in the rare case of the arrow-leaved violet, above referred to. The earliest yellow flowers, like the dandelion and yellow violets, are not fragrant. Later in the season yellow is frequently accompanied with fragrance, as in the evening primrose, the yellow lady's-slipper, horned bladderwort, and others.

My readers probably remember that on a former occasion I have mildly taken the poet Bryant to task for leading his readers to infer that the early yellow violet is sweet-scented. In view of the capriciousness of the perfume of certain of our wild flowers, I have during the past few years tried industriously to convict myself of error in respect to this flower. The round-leaved yellow violet was one of the earliest and most abundant wild flowers in the woods where my youth was passed, and whither I still make annual pilgrimages. I have pursued it on mountains and in lowlands, in "beechen woods" and amid the hemlocks; and while, with respect to its earliness, it overtakes the hepatica in the latter part of April, as do also the dog's-tooth violet and the claytonia, yet the first hepaticas, where the two plants grow side by side, bloom about a week before the first violet. And I have yet to find one that has an odor that could be called a perfume. A handful of them, indeed, has a faint, bitterish smell, not unlike that of the dandelion in quality; but if every flower that has a smell is sweet-scented, then every bird that makes a noise is a songster.

On the occasion above referred to, I also dissented from Lowell's statement, in "Al Fresco," that in early summer the dandelion blooms, in general, with the buttercup and the clover. I am aware that such criticism of the poets is small game, and not worth the powder. General truth, and not specific fact, is what we are to expect of the poets. Bryant's "Yellow Violet" poem is tender and appropriate, and such as only a real lover and observer of nature could feel or express; and Lowell's "Al Fresco" is full of the luxurious feeling of early summer, and this is, of course, the main thing; a good reader cares for little else; I care for little else myself. But when you take your coin to the assay office, it must be weighed and tested, and in the comments referred to I (unwisely, perhaps) sought to smelt this gold of the poets in the naturalist's pot, to see what alloy of error I could detect in it. Were the poems true to their last word? They were not, and much subsequent investigation has only confirmed my first analysis. The general truth is on my side, and the specific fact, if such exists in this case, on the side of the poets. It is possible that there may be a fragrant yellow violet, as an exceptional occurrence, like that of the sweet-scented, arrow-leaved species above referred to, and that in some locality it may have bloomed before the hepatica; also that Lowell may have seen a belated dandelion or two in June, amid the clover and the buttercups; but, if so, they were the exception, and not the rule, — the specific or accidental fact, and not the general truth.

Dogmatism about nature, or about anything else, very often turns out to be an ungrateful cur that bites the hand that reared it. I speak from experience. I was once quite certain that the honey-bee did not work upon the blossoms of the trailing arbutus, but while walking in the woods one April day I came upon a spot of arbutus swarming with honey-bees. They were so eager for it that they crawled under the leaves and the moss to get at the blossoms, and refused on the instant the hive-honey which I happened to have with me, and which I offered them. I had had this flower under observation more than twenty years, and had never before seen it visited by honey-bees. The same season I saw them for the first time working upon the flower of bloodroot and of adder's-tongue. Hence I would not undertake to say again what flowers bees do not work upon. Virgil implies that they work upon the violet, and for aught I know they may. I have seen them very busy on the blossoms of the white oak, though this is not considered a honey or pollen yielding tree. From the smooth sumac they reap a harvest in midsummer, and in March they get a good grist of pollen from the skunk-cabbage.

I presume, however, it would be safe to say that there is a species of smilax with an unsavory name that the bee does not visit, *Smilax herbacea*. The production of this plant is a curious freak of nature. I find it growing along the fences where one would look for wild roses or the sweetbrier; its recurving or climbing stem, its glossy, deep-green, heart-shaped leaves, its clustering umbels of small greenish yellow flowers, making it very pleasing to the eye; but to examine it closely one must positively hold his nose. It would be too cruel a joke to offer it to any person not acquainted with it to smell. It is like the vent of a charnel-house. It is first cousin to the trilliums, among the prettiest of our native wild flowers, and the same bad blood crops out in the purple trillium or birthroot.

Nature will include the disagreeable and repulsive also. I have seen the phallic fungus growing in June under a rosebush. There was the rose, and beneath it, springing from the same mould, was this diabolical offering to Priapus. With the perfume of the roses into the open window came the stench of this hideous parody, as if in mockery. I removed it, and another appeared in the same place shortly afterward. The earthman was rampant and insulting. Pan is not dead yet. At least he still makes a ghastly sign here and there in nature.

The good observer of nature exists in fragments, a trait here and a trait there. Each person sees what it concerns him to see. The fox-hunter knows pretty well the ways and habits of the fox, but on any other subject he is apt to mislead you. He comes to see only fox traits in whatever he looks upon. The bee-hunter will follow the bee, but lose the bird. The farmer notes what affects his crops and his earnings, and little else. Common people, St. Pierre says, observe without reasoning, and the learned reason without observing. If one could apply to the observation of nature the sense

and skill of the South American *rastreador*, or
trailer, how much he would track home! This
man's eye, according to the accounts of travelers,
is keener than a hound's scent. A fugitive can no
more elude him than he can elude fate. His perceptions are said to be so keen that the displace-
ment of a leaf or pebble, or the bending down of
a spear of grass, or the removal of a little dust from
the fence, is enough to give him the clew. He
sees the half-obliterated footprints of a thief in the
sand, and carries the impression in his eye till a
year afterward, when he again detects the same
footprint in the suburbs of a city, and the culprit
is tracked home and caught. I knew a man blind
from his youth who not only went about his own
neighborhood without a guide, turning up to his
neighbor's gate or door as unerringly as if he had
the best of eyes, but who would go many miles on
an errand to a new part of the country. He seemed
to carry a map of the township in the bottom of
his feet, a most minute and accurate survey. He
never took the wrong road, and he knew the right
house when he had reached it. He was a miller
and fuller, and ran his mill at night while his sons
ran it by day. He never made a mistake with his
customers' bags or wool, knowing each man's by the
sense of touch. He frightened a colored man whom
he detected stealing, as if he had seen out of the
back of his head. Such facts show one how deli-

cate and sensitive a man's relation to outward nature through his bodily senses may become. Heighten it a little more, and he could forecast the weather and the seasons, and detect hidden springs and minerals. A good observer has something of this delicacy and quickness of perception. All the great poets and naturalists have it. Agassiz traces the glaciers like a *rastreador;* and Darwin misses no step that the slow but tireless gods of physical change have taken, no matter how they cross or retrace their course. In the obscure fish-worm he sees an agent that has kneaded and leavened the soil like giant hands.

One secret of success in observing nature is capacity to take a hint; a hair may show where a lion is hid. One must put this and that together, and value bits and shreds. Much alloy exists with the truth. The gold of nature does not look like gold at the first glance. It must be smelted and refined in the mind of the observer. And one must crush mountains of quartz and wash hills of sand to get it. To know the indications is the main matter. People who do not know the secret are eager to take a walk with the observer to find where the mine is that contains such nuggets, little knowing that his ore-bed is but a gravel-heap to them. How insignificant appear most of the facts which one sees in his walks, in the life of the birds, the flowers, the animals, or in the phases of the landscape, or the look of the sky!—insignificant until they are put through some mental or emotional process and their true value appears. The diamond looks like a pebble until it is cut. One goes to Nature only for hints and half truths. Her facts are crude until you have absorbed them or translated them. Then the ideal steals in and lends a charm in spite of one. It is not so much what we see as what the thing seen suggests. We all see about the same; to one it means much, to another little. A fact that has passed through the mind of man, like lime or iron that has passed through his blood, has some quality or property superadded or brought out that it did not possess before. You may go to the fields and the woods, and gather fruit that is ripe for the palate without any aid of yours, but you cannot do this in science or in art. Here truth must be disentangled and interpreted, — must be made in the image of man. Hence all good observation is more or less a refining and transmuting process, and the secret is to know the crude material when you see it. I think of Wordsworth's lines:—

> "The mighty world
> Of eye and ear, both what they half create, and what
> perceive;"

which is as true in the case of the naturalist as of the poet; both "half create" the world they describe.

Darwin does something to his facts as well as Tennyson to his. Before a fact can become poetry, it must pass through the heart or the imagination of the poet; before it can become science, it must pass through the understanding of the scientist. Or one may say, it is with the thoughts and half thoughts that the walker gathers in the woods and fields, as with the common weeds and coarser wild flowers which he plucks for a bouquet, — wild carrot, purple aster, moth mullein, sedge, grass, etc. : they look common and uninteresting enough there in the fields, but the moment he separates them from the tangled mass, and brings them indoors, and places them in a vase, say of some choice glass, amid artificial things, — behold, how beautiful! They have an added charm and significance at once; they are defined and identified, and what was common and familiar becomes unexpectedly attractive. The writer's style, the quality of mind he brings, is the vase in which his commonplace impressions and incidents are made to appear so beautiful and significant.

Man can have but one interest in nature, namely, to see himself reflected or interpreted there, and we quickly neglect both poet and philosopher who fail to satisfy, in some measure, this feeling.

BIBLIOGRAPHY

Barrus, Clara. *Whitman and Burroughs: Comrades.* 1931. Reprint. Port Washington, N.Y.: Kennikat Press, 1968.

————. *The Life and Letters of John Burroughs.* 2 vols. Boston and New York: Houghton Mifflin and Co., 1925.

Bashō. *The Narrow Road to the Deep North.* Translated by Nobuyuki Yuasa. Middlesex, England: Penguin Books, 1968.

Burroughs, John. *Notes on Walt Whitman as Poet and Person.* New York: American News Co., 1867.

————. *The Writings of John Burroughs.* Riverby Edition. 23 vols. Boston and New York: Houghton Mifflin and Co., 1904-1923. Reprint. New York: Russell and Russell, 1968.

————. *The Heart of Burroughs's Journals.* Edited by Clara Barrus. Boston and New York: Houghton Mifflin and Co., 1928.

Emerson, Ralph Waldo. *Nature: A Facsimile of the First Edition.* Introduction by Werner Berthoff. San Francisco: Chandler Publishing Co., 1968.

Foerster, Norman. *Nature in American Literature.* 1923. Reprint. New York: Russell and Russell, 1958.

Howells, William Dean. Rev. of *Wake-Robin*, by John Burroughs. *Atlantic Monthly*, 28 (Aug. 1871), 254.

James, Henry. *Views and Reviews.* Freeport, N.Y.: Books for Libraries Press, [1968].

Kelley, Elizabeth Burroughs. *John Burroughs: Naturalist.* New York: Exposition Press, 1959.

————. *John Burroughs' Slabsides.* Rhinebeck, N.Y.: Moran Printing Co., 1974.

Louis Agassiz Fuertes and the Singular Beauty of Birds. Edited by Frederick George Markham. New York: Harper & Row, 1971.

Perry, Bliss. *The Praise of Folly and Other Papers.* Boston and New York: Houghton Mifflin and Co., 1923.

BIBLIOGRAPHY

Sharp, Dallas Lore. "Fifty Years of John Burroughs," *Atlantic Monthly*, 106 (Nov. 1910), 631-641.

Welker, Robert Henry. *Birds and Men: American Birds in Science, Art, Literature and Conservation, 1800-1900*. Cambridge, Mass.: Harvard University Press, 1955.

Westbrook, Perry D. *John Burroughs*. New York: Twayne Publishers, 1974.

Whitman, Walt. *Leaves of Grass: The First (1855) Edition*. Edited by Malcolm Cowley. New York: Viking Press, 1959.